HOW TO BUDGET

Control Your Money Before It Controls You

M.H. KHAN

Table of Contents

INTRODUCTION

THIS BOOK IS CHOCK-FULL of solid advice—plus tips and tricks—to help you reach your financial goals, no matter what your current financial situation is and no matter how lofty your goals are. Okay, so you may not be able to retire at age forty, especially if you're currently thirty-nine years old. But you can live a life free from the stress of dodging creditors and wondering how you're going to make your rent or mortgage payment, even in today's rocky economy.

Imagine the following as your future life. Every two weeks, on a Friday, your paycheck is directly deposited to your bank: a portion to your retirement account, a portion of your savings account, and a portion of your checking account. During the weekend, you pay the bills that will come due before your next paycheck—and

not only do you have enough money to cover all those bills, but you also withdraw some spending money for the next two weeks.

Meanwhile, the money in your retirement account is increasing, and the money in your savings account—after the six months' salary you always leave in there for emergencies—will allow you to pay cash for the sofa you've had your eye on, that vacation you're going to take next summer, the baby you're expecting later this year, or any other great use for your money you can think of.

Sound impossible? It's not. With careful budgeting—and a commitment to live within that budget—your life can be exactly like the one just described. Between now and then, though, you may have to radically rein in your spending, aggressively pay down your debts, and begin to save. If your situation is serious enough, you may have to cease all spending for the next six months (or more). But at the end of that time, you'll be well on your way toward developing a cushion of savings in the bank; planning for a new home, your retirement, and/or your child's college education; and having enough income to meet your needs each month.

To get started, first, you'll want to determine which part of your current spending plan is a high priority. Then, you'll want to understand your overall financial picture, as it is now. Don't shy away from this step, even if you know that your financial picture is very, very bad.

Knowing the full breadth of your assets and financial obligations helps you establish a budget that will change your financial picture from bleak to promising. If you're having trouble balancing your personal budget, consider putting a temporary moratorium on spending. You'll likely also want to cut down on your existing financial obligations, small and large; immediately tackle your debt; and, if necessary, find ways to add income so that you can get out of debt even faster.

Thinking about buying a house (and yes, you can save up enough for a 20 percent down payment)? Are you saving for your child's education? Found yourself separated or divorced, and aren't sure what financial step to take next? Want to plan for retirement? Having trouble staying motivated? It's all here.

Thanks for downloading this book. It's my firm belief that it will provide you with all the answers to your questions

CHAPTER 1

WHAT IS BUDGETING—AND WHY DO YOU NEED TO DO IT?

Budgeting. The very word can bring tears to your eyes. Yet, if you have any financial goals—any at all, from being debt-free to buying a house to retiring in comfort—budgeting is the single activity that will simplify and improve your life.

Realize What a Budget Is

Establishing a budget is the act of deciding how much of your money you're going to spend on one item, how much on another, and so on before you're actually in the position of spending the money. Sticking to a budget is the act of following through on those decisions. Creating a budget isn't easy, and sticking to your budget is extremely difficult.

You have to stick to the budget; the budget itself doesn't have the power to do that for you—it's just a piece of paper. Only you can decide that you're willing to stick to a lower level of spending, work at another job to add income, or both.

The trick is to focus on the word "realistic." Without doing any research, you may decide that you're going to spend $200 per month on food. But if you've never spent less than $500 per month on food, you'll blow your budget right out of the water the first week. Instead, before you begin deciding on the numbers in your budget, you'll need to assess your current situation fully, take a hard look at where you can cut back your financial obligations (both large and small), restructure your debt (if necessary), and see whether you can add income. Only then are you ready to decide realistically where every penny will be spent.

Recognize What a Budget Isn't

A budget isn't a straitjacket that keeps you from really living. On the contrary, a budget that you stick to can be your ticket to living the life you imagine. Living within a strict budget isn't easy, but neither is being heavily in debt, worrying about how to pay for your expenses, and living with the guilt that goes with spending money you don't have. You've already done the hard part by living with financial insecurity; even though living within a budget isn't fun, it won't be any harder than that.

Keep in mind, though, that simply establishing a budget isn't the answer to your financial woes. Establishing even the world's greatest budget won't make any of your financial goals a reality unless you stick to the budget and follow through.

Understand Financial Goals

People establish budgets because they have financial goals that are not being met. They may not realize that they have any goals at all—they may just be tired of bill collectors calling—but everyone who establishes a budget has at least one unmet financial goal. For example, you may want to:

- Be able to pay all your bills from your paycheck—and maybe have a little left over
- Buy or build a house
- Save for retirement
- Pay off your credit cards and never get into debt again
- Give more money to your church or to other nonprofits
- Be your own boss
- Take a vacation every year
- Stop hearing from the hospital about your unpaid medical bills
- Buy a new—or at least newer—car
- Stay home with your baby
- Remodel part of your house
- Adopt a child
- Finance at least part of your child's college education
- Overhaul your wardrobe
- Rebuild your credit
- Find a way to care for your aging parents
- Have some cosmetic surgery done
- Take a leave of absence from your job to write a novel
- Go back to school and begin a new career

- Open a coffee shop

Are any of these your goals? If so, budgeting will get you there, regardless of whether the odds seem impossible right now. Even if you're stuck in a job you don't like, desperately want to go back to school, have to take care of an aging parent, and have $45,000 in credit card debt, you can meet your financial goals—just as others have done before you. With a good budget, a little patience, and a whole lot of determination, you'll eventually get there.

Not convinced that you need a budget? Here's a test to determine whether you need one: Do you have even one unmet financial goal? Whether you want to put meals on the table for your family, buy a great dress for your high school reunion, see a credit card bill that says your balance is $0, or take on any of the other goals listed earlier, no goal is too big or too small. And if you're having trouble reaching your goal, you need a budget. Period.

Look at a Sample Budget

Meet Sylvie, age thirty-eight, whose budget we're going to peek at to see how this process works. Sylvie has worked at the same company for eight years, breaking into a middle-management position last year. She bought a comfortable house four years ago, has a car payment on a three-year-old car, owes $6,800 in credit card debt, has some money in savings, is a single parent with two children, and participates in her company's 401(k) plan, which matches 50 percent of her contribution. Sylvie usually has enough money to pay the bills every two weeks, although the kids' growing expenses are starting to pressure the family's income.

The first step in developing a budget is to decide what you want your finances to allow you to do in life. To this end, Sylvie has the following goals:

- Help her kids pay for college. She has decided she'll pay for half the expenses at one of the three large public universities in her state (currently $18,500 per year for tuition, fees, room, and board) or put that same amount toward a private or out-of-state college, knowing that her children will be eligible for scholarships and financial aid.
- Pay off the credit card in nine months. Get the balance to zero, and then if it's used at all, pay it off in full every month.
- Retire from her company at age fifty (in twelve years), and open a coffee shop in a coastal town she fell in love with a few years ago. She'd like to buy whatever building her shop is in and live above it: she estimates $550,000 for the building and start-up fees, but that price will surely rise in twelve years.
- Put away a $50,000 safety net over the next twelve years. This money would be for emergencies only, not to be touched for any other expenses.

Sample Income

Sylvie's biweekly income after taxes (which provides her with a refund of about $1,250 per year), company sponsored medical and dental insurance (at a cost of $155 per pay period), company-sponsored life insurance for $250,000 of coverage ($22 per pay period), and 401(k) contributions ($75 per pay period, matched at 50 percent of the company) is $2,104. Because there are twenty-six biweekly paychecks in a year, this comes to $54,704 per year or $4,559 per month. Sylvie also currently has $1,700 in savings.

Remember to use these numbers only as a sample. If yours are much higher or much lower, that's perfectly okay. Your situation is unique, and no one else's budgeting numbers should mean a whole lot to you.

Sample Ways to Reduce Debt

Sylvie's monthly obligations and her monthly income are well balanced, so she's usually able to pay all her bills. Her credit card debt comes from those months when expenses were unexpected, and her savings comes from those (rare) months when there was a little extra. However, Sylvie has considerable financial goals, and in order to free up enough money to save for them, some of her current expenses must be eliminated. Here's what Sylvie decides to do:

- Keep the car and car payment. After paying off the car in one year, continue to drive it for several years after that, putting the same $382 into savings each month for the next car. No monthly savings at present, but for big savings in the future.
- Cut down on utilities, shopping around for a better family cell phone plan and installing a programmable thermostat (although it has an initial cost of $46) to save on her gas and electricity bills. Estimated monthly savings: $83.

- Spend a maximum of $125 per week on groceries. Also, limit eating out to take-out once a week. Estimated monthly savings: $175.
- Eliminate the small stuff. Keep coffee shop visits to once per week; borrow magazines, eBooks, and movies from the library; and otherwise reduce monthly spending money to $150 ($100 for both kids' allowances; $50 for Sylvie). Monthly savings: $50.
- Investigate car insurance options to lower annual insurance costs by $400. Monthly savings: $33.
- Limit vacation spending to $1,500 per year by being creative. Monthly savings: $192.
- Allow each member of the family $600 per year to spend on clothing and shoes (teaching the kids budgeting skills in the process). Any more than that and the kids will have to use their allowances or get part-time jobs. Monthly savings: $117.

TOTAL Monthly Savings: $650

Meeting Goals for This Sample

Now, Sylvie must increase her monthly savings and investments to meet her financial goals:

- Refinance the mortgage on the house at 4.2 percent for fifteen years, paying it off in twelve (so that it can be sold, debt-free, to help pay for the coffee shop building and start-up expenses, which will then be mortgaged for fifteen years). Monthly increase: $350.

- Pay off the credit card in nine months. Monthly increase: $725.
- Save for college in a Section 529 fund. Monthly new expense: $800.
- Put away a safety net of $50,000 over the next twelve years. Monthly new expense: $335.

TOTAL monthly increase: $2,150

Revisit the Sample Goals and Priorities

Sylvie will be $1,560 short each month, so it's time to revisit her listed goals to see which can be changed. Here's her revised list of goals:

- Help the kids pay for college, as previously described.
- Pay off the credit card, but begin saving for the kids' college fund only when it's paid off. This will actually pay off the card in five months, not nine!
- Retire from the company at age 54 (in sixteen years) and open her coffee shop.
- Put away a $40,000 nest egg over the next sixteen years.
- These changes mean the following financial adjustments:
- Refinance the mortgage on the house at 4.8 percent, for thirty years, with the understanding that in eight years (when college savings will no longer be necessary), the money currently used to save for college will be redirected to the mortgage. Making those large extra payments toward the mortgage after the kids finish college will result in the

mortgage being paid off in eighteen years, not thirty. Reduces monthly shortfall by $560.

- Put away $200 per month (instead of $335) to create a nest egg over the next sixteen years. Reduces monthly shortfall by $135.
- Delay Section 529 college funds by five months, using that money plus funds from savings to pay off credit card debt. Reduces monthly shortfall by $800.

TOTAL monthly increase from current spending: $65

Sylvie has created a working budget since she has enough cushion between her income and her current expenses to incorporate that $65 per month in additional spending/saving. It won't be easy to cut back, but the family does still have some discretionary spending money, the kids' educational savings are in good shape, and Sylvie will own her coffee shop in that beautiful town in just sixteen years.

Think about Your Long-Term Financial Goals

The first step in your own budgeting process is to think about your financial priorities and goals.

Decide What's Important to You

A lot of people wish they could meet their financial goals in the future and still live well in the present. You may wonder why you can't retire at forty-five, and until then, still, eat out every day, live in a luxurious house, and lease a BMW. After all, your neighbors live in a large house, drive expensive cars, eat at nice restaurants, wear the latest fashions, send their kids to private colleges, and have a boat—they don't appear to be giving up anything. Perhaps they're not, and they're much wealthier than you thought. Or (and this is more likely), they are drowning in debt, aren't working toward their financial goals, and aren't doing nearly as well as you think.

Keep in mind that you can live quite well without really having the means to do so. You used to be able to buy a house with very little money down and (for luxurious homes) stretch out the payments for as long as fifty years, and many people are still in those mortgages. You can lease a luxury automobile.

You can borrow money to pay for your kids' college education. You can buy clothes and boats, take vacations, and eat in fine restaurants using credit cards, paying the money back very, very slowly. When your credit card bills get too high, you can borrow against the equity in your house to pay them off, or you can open up new credit card accounts. This is the way many Americans live—on borrowed money. But at some point, debt catches up with everyone.

Since you're reading this book, you've decided you no longer want to live that way. Instead, you're willing to give up something now to have your financial goals met in the future. Exactly what you give up, though, is strictly up to you; you decide which expenses are most important right now. Don't let advertisements, your friends, and coworkers, or your desire to keep up with the neighbors affect your priorities. Only you can decide what's important to you.

You may decide, for example, that life is too short to cut back on vacations, or that instead of spending time cooking, you want to be able to eat out every day and spend that time socializing with your family instead. That's perfectly okay. But in the process, you may, for example, also decide to move to a smaller house—or cut expenses less drastically.

Don't think you can have it all because chances are, and you can't. But you can retain what's important to you while giving up what's much less important.

Make Your Financial Goals a Reality

Do you want to be debt-free? Do you want to pay for your child's college education? Do you want to retire comfortably at age sixty-five, or at age forty-five? This section helps you decide and understand what you'll have to do to make those goals a reality.

Your financial goals drive your budget and give you a reason to stick to it. Without written goals that every decision-maker in your household agrees to, you'll have a difficult time resisting spending money whenever the urge strikes.

Use WORKSHEET 1-1 to write down all the financial goals you can think of. Whether you have just one goal or you end up with too many to fit on this worksheet, you're doing just fine. (For now, ignore the "Priority" and "Monthly Amount" columns.)

WORKSHEET 1-1
YOUR FINANCIAL GOALS

Goals	Date	Amount needed	Priority 1-5	Monthly amount
		$		$
		$		$
		$		$
		$		$
		$		$
		$		$
		$		$

Now go back and assign a priority to each financial goal, with the numbers five through one meaning something like the following:

5: You would be miserable if you didn't achieve this financial goal by the proposed date.

4: You'd be very disappointed if you came to the end of your life and hadn't achieved this financial goal.

3: You would have some regrets if you didn't achieve this financial goal, but it wouldn't bother you for long.

2: While this goal is important, you have others that are far more important.

1: This is a fun goal to think about, but you're not really committed to it.

The reality is that you may not have enough income, or you may have too many expenses that you can't cut to meet all of your financial goals. With a prioritized list, however, you can decide which goals you want to attack right now and which ones can wait.

You have just one more step, and that's to turn your financial goals into monthly amounts. Simply divide the total amount needed by the number of months between now and your goal's due date. For a goal that you want to complete two years from now, for example, divide the amount of money needed by twenty-four to get the monthly amount.

If you have a decision-making partner in your finances, each of you should fill out a worksheet independently, assign your own priorities, then share worksheets with each other. You'll have to compromise on some goals, and you may have to sit down several times to work out details, but you'll emerge with shared financial goals you can both look forward to.

Because you'll earn interest on your savings during that twenty-four months, you'll actually have a bit more than the amount needed, but because many savings accounts earn less than 1 percent interest, just keep it simple by forgetting about interest for now.

CHAPTER 2

PRIORITIZE YOUR SPENDING

How much do you spend every day, and which of those expenses are important to you? Can you stop spending altogether (a temporary situation, but a good technique to use when spending is out of control)? This chapter will help you prioritize how you spend.

Why Not Spending Is the Key to Budgeting

You have two ways to free up money for your financial goals: making more or spending less. Neither one is better than the other, right? Wrong! If 22 percent of your income goes to state and federal taxes, then for every extra dollar you earn, you have only 78 cents to pay off debt or save for the future. But if you can save a dollar of your expenses, you can apply all of it to your debt or put it into savings or investments.

Through direct deposit, your employer deposits your paycheck into your bank account. Instead of a check, you receive a notice from your employer that the deposit has been made. If you have this option, take it. You're more likely to save than spend if you use this feature!

Total Your Daily Expenses

The method of totaling your expenses in worksheet 2-1 is simple: You either report what you spent last week—day by day, expense by expense—or you start fresh this week and record every expenditure going forward. If you record your expenses this coming week, be sure you don't try to be "good" and spend less than you usually do.

Monday		Tuesday		Wednesday		Thursday	
Item	Amount	Item	Amount	Item	Amount	Item	Amount
	$		$		$		$
	$		$		$		$
	$		$		$		$
	$		$		$		$
	$		$		$		$
Total	$		$		$		$

Categorize and Prioritize Your Daily Expenses

Review your daily lists, and categorize them in the most logical way you can: coffee, breakfasts, apps, lunches, eBooks, clothing, toiletries, groceries, and so on. Use

WORKSHEET 2-2 to record your findings. Ignore the "Priority" column until you've listed all of your expenses by category.

Category	Amount	Priority 1-5
	$	
	$	
	$	
	$	
Total	$	

Now go back and assign a priority to each category—5 being something you absolutely can't live without, and one meaning you'd barely notice if you no longer spent money on this one. Your priorities don't necessarily mean that you will continue to spend this money in the exact same way.

Assess Your Monthly Expenses

Recording your monthly expenses in a worksheet 2-3 through 2-6 works just like your daily one. For these monthly worksheets, your best bet is to go back through your receipts and bank statements, and also use your memory. If on the other hand, you simply record all your monthly expenses starting in January, you'll understand your January expenses on January 31, but you won't have a clear picture of your December spending until a year from now, and that's valuable time that you could be using to reach your financial goals. Instead, to more quickly get a clear picture of your monthly expense, dig out your bank statements, receipts, and so on.

Be sure not to double up on daily and monthly expenses. If you've already recorded a certain expense on your daily expense sheets, do not record it here.

Date	Item	Amount	Date	Item	Amount	Date	Item	Amount
		$			$			$
		$			$			$
		$			$			$
		$			$			$
		$			$			$
		$			$			$

Categorize and Prioritize Your Monthly Expenses

In the same way that you worked with the daily worksheets, group your monthly expenses into categories (utilities, rent, insurance, etc.) and add them to Don't let once-in-a-while expenses catch you off guard. To be sure you've thought of everything, go through last year's bank statements, receipts, tax return, e-mails, and/or calendar to jog your memory about what you spent money on.

Prioritize What You Spend Money On

You should now have a list of your expenses by category, with a priority attached to each one. If you have enough income to reach all of your financial goals and still spend money the way you currently do, you won't need this prioritized list, though it's likely you won't meet your financial goals if you continue to spend.

Use this list to choose the areas that you absolutely do not want to cut back on (these are the items that have a priority rating of 5). If you have too many items with a high priority to meet your financial goals, sub prioritize those items, so that you come up with just a few. Spending on these items will make all the cutbacks easier to swallow.

Keep in mind that you are the only one who can determine your priorities. If you would rather drive an old car so that you can still afford to buy organic fruits and vegetables, do it.

CHAPTER 3

ASSESS YOUR CURRENT FINANCIAL SITUATION

In order to establish a budget, you have to understand your financial situation right now. That way, you can see exactly how far you have to go before you reach your goals. This chapter contains tips for identifying your financial goals, your income (money coming into you), and your financial obligations (outflows of money).

Your Financial Situation Is Important

Before you can create a budget, you have to know every detail of your financial situation. Although you probably understand in general how much you spend and where you spend it, you may be amazed at how much you actually spend on certain items that don't seem like they could add up so fast.

The exercises here are designed to give you an unflinchingly honest appraisal of where you stand. If you have a tendency to become overwhelmed easily, identify a friend you can phone for support, plan to take breaks for a walk outside, and keep upbeat music playing in the background as you put together your income and expenses.

Determine Your Income and Other Assets

Your income includes any money that comes into your possession and can be counted on in the near future. Your paycheck is considered income, but income isn't limited only to a paycheck you receive from your employer. It's also a disability payment, a welfare check, a Social Security check, alimony, child support, self-employment income from a small business, and so on. Whatever money comes in—money that you can count on—is what you want to consider as income.

Keep in mind that income is considered income only if you can count on it. So getting lucky at the horse track this weekend is not income—because you could just as easily lose the same amount of money at the track.

Identify all your sources of income, add them up, and figure them on an annual basis. you can calculate all of your income for a given pay period and multiply it to get an annual amount. Be sure to write down the net amount of each paycheck—that's the amount you take home after the taxes, insurance, union dues, and other items are deducted.

You'll then multiply your paycheck to get your annual income: biweekly paychecks are multiplied by 26, semimonthly by 24, and so on.

26

If you get paid monthly, you may have a harder time than most with your budget. The amount of your check may seem like a lot at the beginning of the month, but three or four weeks later, your expenses may have exceeded that check. A strict weekly budget can really help.

Remember that this is not projected income. Don't write down the income you think you'll have after a promotion or other situation; what you want to look at is exactly how much money you have to work with right now.

Calculate Your Financial Obligations

In this section, you look at the debt and living expenses that you pay each year. These range from your monthly rent or mortgage payment to a car payment or lease, utility bills (including your cell phone), food, entertainment, contributions to charities, gifts (holidays, weddings, birthdays), alimony payments, credit card payments, and store charge-card payments.

Don't try to be "good" when listing your current expenses. Base this list on what you've done in the past, not what you'd like to do in the future. If you've spent $150 each of the last five months in the Target clearance section, you may not be able to break that habit cold turkey.

Write Down Full Debt Amounts

Write down and indicate the total amount you owe on credit cards and store charge cards; don't write only the minimum payments. Here's why: Suppose you owe $5,000 to a credit card company, but rather than saying that you owe them $5,000 this month, your bill says that you have to make a payment of $65. That's

your monthly payment, right? Wrong. Credit card and store charge-card companies are in the business of making money. Did you know that if you make the minimum monthly payment, you might be paying on that $5,000 for ten or fifteen years? And that's without charging even one more item to your account in all that time! Paying the minimum is never going to help you get your financial situation under control.

Remember that "obligations" refer to any money you owe anyone. You may think your grandma has forgotten all about that $5,000 she loaned you to buy a car, but write it down anyway. Grandma may have a better memory than you think!

Gather Information

You probably know how much your rent or mortgage payment is off the top of your head, but you may not know exactly how much your utility bills have been. To find that information, look back through your bank statements and receipts. If you can't come up with the amount, give your utility company a call. If you ask, they'll probably e-mail you free copies of your bills for the last year.

Average Out Utility Payments

It's important to look at all of your utility payments—not just the one for last month—because some of them might change from month to month. For example, your electric bill may get much higher in the summer if you live in an area where air conditioning is critical to your comfort. Likewise, your gas bill may rise sharply in the winter if you live in an area that has low temperatures at that time of year. On the other hand, your cell, cable, water, and other utilities may not change at all.

To figure out how much your average electric bill is, add up your last twelve monthly payments to the electric company and divide by twelve. This will give you the average amount that you pay each month.

Remember Periodic Expenses

Remember to consider the expenses that people tend to forget because they come due only every six or twelve months:

- Auto and life insurance
- Vehicle excise tax (if your state has one)
- Car repair and maintenance
- Homeowner's or renter's insurance
- Association fees
- Property taxes
- House repair and maintenance
- Contributions
- Tuition
- Gifts (holiday, birthday, wedding)
- Events to attend (such as weddings and holiday gatherings)
- Vacations
- Medical deductibles and other expenses

Unlike the income worksheet, for this worksheet, do try to anticipate any expense that may come up in the next twelve months, for you and your family. If your best friend who lives 2,000 miles away is probably going to get married, calculate the cost of that trip, the clothes you'll need, the gift you'll buy, and so on.

If, as part of your monthly mortgage payment, you pay one-sixth or one-twelfth of your homeowner's insurance and property taxes, which are then stored in an escrow account until they are due, write down your total monthly mortgage payment, and then leave the lines for your homeowner's insurance and property taxes blank.

Put Your Income and Financial Obligations Together

Now compare your income-to-obligations ratio

After you've completed determining your income, let's assess how you did.

Ten or Greater: Your Income Far Exceeds Your Debts

Assuming you were honest in your assessment of your income and obligations, you should have no trouble establishing a budget you can live with. If you can't seem to come up with enough money to pay the bills each month, or your credit card debts are growing, find tools for tracking your daily, weekly, and monthly expenses to get a handle on where your money is going.

Zero to Nine: Your Income Just Barely Exceeds Your Debts

What this means is that, on an annual basis, you just barely get by. If you have trouble paying your bills each month, you may have one of two problems: Either your expenses are actually higher than you think, or you may have cash-flow problems (discussed in the following section).

Negative One to Negative Ten: Your Debt Just Barely Exceeds Your Income

Many people are living just a little above their means. In order to do this, they use credit cards, store charge cards, home equity loans, short-term loans, and so on to make ends meet. The problem is that if you're short $300 per month and use credit cards to pay for groceries or clothing, at the end of the year, you'll be $3,600 in debt. Ten years later, given most credit card interest rates, you'll be over $80,000 in debt!

Negative Ten or Less: Your Debt Far Exceeds Your Income

This situation often occurs during in-between times in life. For example, when you're in college or have just graduated, you're in between living with your parents' help and working full time to pay your own expenses, but you may still have the same spending patterns that you had when your parents were paying all your expenses. You may also have a lot of debt due to a layoff or medical leave, or when you have one huge debt hanging over your head, such as a school loan or unexpected medical bill.

The primary reason people get into debt is that they spend more than they earn. Simple, right? Well, not really. For most people, income is fixed—you know how much your paycheck will be. But expenses can vary greatly, depending on, for example, whether you needed dental work, how often you eat out, whether you spend a lot on a big sale, and whether you go over your cell minutes.

If you have more obligations than income, you're not alone. The average U.S. household has over $15,000 in credit card debt, which means that millions of Americans are likely to be in this exact situation, using credit cards as a way to keep up with expenses. If you find yourself with more obligations than income, you need to pare down some of those obligations, so you have enough income to pay your bills every month.

Identify Potential Cash-Flow Problems

Often, if your income just barely exceeds your obligations, on paper you look like you'll get by just fine, but in reality, you may find yourself coming up short at certain times of the year.

Suppose, for example, that you have an income of $36,000 per year (after taxes) and $35,000 in obligations. A problem often arises when one of your periodic expenses, such as car insurance, is due. Technically, you might have enough income from January to December to cover your car insurance, but if your insurance bill arrives in February, you may not have had time to put enough money into savings each month to cover this expense. This is called a cash-flow problem, and to manage this situation successfully, you have to reduce your debt (or increase your income) to the point where you're living far enough below your income that you don't have trouble paying your large periodic expenses. See debt-reduction ideas and tips on increasing your income later in the book.

Take a Break if You Need It

If your financial picture is rather bleak, this has probably been difficult for you. Establishing a written budget that you're going to be living with for the next few months and years probably isn't going to be any easier. Even if you're the type who likes to plow through, you might want to take a break for a few hours, or overnight.

Don't give up here, though! Just take a short break, inhale deeply, and get ready to change your life for the better.

CHAPTER 4

CREATE A LIVABLE BUDGET

This chapter will help you create—and then evaluate the potential problems with—your first budget. You'll find out what elements are required for living a budgeted life, and then you'll work on your own budget.

Make Your Financial Goals a Reality

The reason you create a budget is that you have financial goals. These may range from buying a motorcycle to owning your own home to saving for retirement.

No matter what your financial situation, you have financial goals, even though you may not think of them that way. If you have a particular lifestyle you want to live, places you want to go, or people you want to help, you have financial goals.

Earlier in this book, there is a sample listing of a wide range of financial goals. Your list may be very different, and should be unique to your distinct set of circumstances. Whatever goals you have, they're right. No one else's goals are appropriate for you, and your set of goals probably isn't right for anyone else.

When you create a budget, you keep all of your financial goals as the central focus, figuring out how to cut your current expenses—or increase your current income—to get you on track to meet those goals. How you decide to cut back or add income will be as unique as your goals are. You may make very different choices than your friends, family, and neighbors do about how and where you'll live. Every decision you make will be specific to your financial goals and your current financial situation, which no one else has to know about or agree with. Just smile when people question your decisions, knowing you have quite a secret!

The secret to financial security is really quite simple. Spend less than you earn, save for the big-ticket items you have your eye on, keep money in the bank for emergencies, and plan for the day when you won't want to—or won't be able to—work as much.

Keep in mind, though, that you may not be able to meet every one of your goals if you also want to maintain your current level of spending. You need to decide which goals are most important to you, and figure out how to prioritize your current expenses.

Spend Less Than You Make

To stay above water financially, you have to spend less than you make. This simple point is the most important principle for constructing and living within a budget.

You simply cannot meet financial goals if you don't live within your means.

Most millionaires don't lead wild and exciting lives. They are ordinary folks who save a lot, are thrifty, and account for every penny. You, too, can amass a small fortune by borrowing eBooks from the library instead of buying them from Amazon, using coupons, making your latte at home, turning down the thermostat, buying long-lasting clothing and shoes, and so on.

Yet many people spend more than they make, and it often starts with just a few bad decisions. Here's an example. A few years ago, a financial advisor on television said that as long as interest rates on new cars stayed at 0 or 1 percent (which car companies were offering at that time), the best financial investment a person could make would be to buy a new car.

In fact, this person suggested that you'd have to be "crazy" not to take advantage of this situation. Hmm. Now, suppose a person watching that program owned a five-year-old car that was completely paid off and ran fine, but after hearing that financial advice, decided to go out and buy a new car. After all, the opportunity for financing this low might never come again.

So, the car owner trades in the perfectly fine car and gets a great deal on a new car, but two months later, the car owner begins to feel the pinch. Monthly car payments went from $0 to $318, and insurance costs went up $168 per year. Before, our car-buying friend always had a bit of extra money every month—enough to put $200 in savings and still have a little left over.

But now, there's nothing to go into savings and no extra cash around. In fact, even in the first few months, the car owner is beginning to put a few groceries on the credit card just to get by. Before long, this one innocent purchase has led to a spiraling financial problem. The car was definitely not the best investment our car owner could have made. A far better decision would have been not to even think about getting a new car until the old one had a problem. The drop in interest rates saved our car owner money, but the car itself—at that particular time—was something our friend didn't need or plan for.

Remember: A product is only a good deal if you've planned for it and can afford it within the context of your other financial goals. Nothing—not low-interest rates, a sale on shoes, the house of your dreams—is ever a good deal if it requires you to spend more than you make.

Spend Money Only on Budgeted Items

After you set up a budget, you spend money only on the items that your budget says you can spend money on. But, while budgets can be constricting, remember that the only person controlling your spending is you—or, to be more exact, your financial goals.

Suppose your primary financial goal is to take a two-month trip to Europe. You're sure that you want to do this, and your budget reflects it. Because you'll be taking time off work without pay, you're saving not only for the trip but also for the income you'll miss while you're gone. You've figured out that if you give up your biscotti and latte every morning, turn down your thermostat, and stop buying clothes for a year; you'll be able to do it. But a couple of months into the year, you decide that this "crazy" budget isn't going to tell you how to run your life and that no one should live without biscotti and latte in a not-very-warm house while wearing old clothes.

What exactly has happened here? Basically, your day-to-day comfort has a higher priority than wanting to go to Europe. So, the budget has to be reworked to reflect this, because if biscotti and clothes aren't in the budget, you can't spend money on them and still make it to Europe. In order to spend euros a year from now, you can't buy items now that you've agreed to give up.

Save for Unexpected Expenses

People often get into financial trouble because they don't expect the unexpected. By intentionally saving for unexpected expenses, you can break this cycle. An unexpected expense may be an auto accident that requires you to pay a deductible or a repair to your home. An "emergency" can also be a planned expense that comes due before you expect it. For example, suppose you had planned to take a vacation later this year, but your best friend is attending a conference in the Bahamas and asks you to go along, stay for free in the hotel, and pay only airfare and food. You might decide that now is a better time to take a vacation because you'll save so much money. However, given your goal to get out and stay out of debt, you don't dare put the trip on credit cards. This trip will be a much easier decision for you if you have money in the bank to borrow against.

Make sure that you have an allotment for savings in your budget, even if it's just $10 per paycheck now, and then work toward eventually saving up to six months' salary for every wage earner in your household.

When you have savings, you have choices. You're never going to feel stuck again. If you're laid off, you have time to find a job you really want. If you've been looking for a new house, and find the perfect one, but the current owners won't wait for you to sell yours first, you can use your savings as a down payment, replacing the savings after you sell your existing house. And on, and on.

The trick to having money available for unexpected expenses is twofold. First, you never dip into your savings unless you're faced with a truly unique situation. A shoe sale at your favorite department store is not a unique situation. The money in your savings account is for that oh-my-gosh-what-am-I-going-to-do-now situation.

The second part of the trick to keeping savings on hand for unexpected events is always to replace it after you use it. If you have six months' salary in the bank and you use one month's salary to make up the difference between your short-term disability pay and your regular pay, when you get back to work full-time, immediately begin replacing that one month's salary.

These two concepts—leaving money in savings for unexpected expenses and replacing any money that you borrow from your savings when unexpected situations arise—are not common in our society. You'll find that some people don't even think they're capable of doing this. If they see they have money in the bank, they'll spend it on whatever they think will make their lives better at that moment. But the truth is, having this security gives you the power to choose, and that's the greatest power you'll ever have—much greater than that 80-inch TV for the Super Bowl.

Revisit Your Goals and Priorities

As you go through the budgeting process, you may find yourself revising your long-term financial goals and your shorter-term spending priorities. And this is a good thing.

Suppose, for example, that you have the following goals: Save for a down payment on a house in two years; buy new furniture for your house when you move in; and within two years, increase savings so that it equals six months' worth of income. You also have your eye on buying a new car next year, and you've recently added this to your list of goals.

Suppose that with your current income, you spend nearly everything you make. Well, in order to save $30,000 for a down payment on a house in two years, you're going to need to save roughly $1,250 per month. The furniture is going to cost $350 for two years, saving six months' salary is going to require $900 a month for two years, and the new car, minus the trade-in on your existing car, will take $1,200 a month for a year. Altogether, this is $3,700 a month. Unless you're currently living an incredibly lavish lifestyle, the chance of being able to cut $3,700 out of your current spending is slim.

You have two options. You can find a way to make more money by getting a second job, doing freelance work, starting your own part-time business, working overtime, or finding a new job that pays more money. That's one way to meet your goals, but keep in mind that whenever you work more hours, you give up something very precious—time. If you have the time to spend, if you are planning to work the extra hours only for a short while, and if working more hours isn't going to jeopardize your health, wreak havoc on your relationship with your kids, or take you away from a hobby that you love, perhaps it will be okay. But if you have to commit to this lifestyle for ten years, you may find it unacceptable.

Isn't re-evaluating the same thing as selling out?

No. Re-evaluating your budget isn't unusual and doesn't mean you've sold out. Instead, it's the only way to generate a budget that will actually work for you.

The other option is to go back and revisit your spending priorities and financial goals. Even if you've cut your expenses as much as you think you can, maybe you can still cut back some more. You may have decided that talking on the phone at any time is a priority, so you've purchased an unlimited-minutes plan. But perhaps you could talk more during free weekend minutes, reduce the minutes in your plan, and free up $30 or $40 per month.

You may also decide to re-evaluate your goals. Perhaps, for example, you decide to buy the house in four years instead of two, which gives you much more time to save for the down payment and the furniture. Perhaps, because both the house and the phone calls are important enough, you can make do with your existing car for several more years. Perhaps you keep working toward getting six months' salary in the bank but stretch that goal out to ten years instead of two. It's all up to you and your priorities.

Generate a Budget You Can Stick To

This section walks you through the steps for generating your own budget.

Start with Your Goals

If you haven't yet written down your goals, you must start there. See Chapter 1 for a worksheet that will help you generate your long-term financial goals, and then return here. You'll need to know your goals before you can establish a budget.

To be useful, your goals must be in financial terms, with actual dollar amounts attached, and must have set deadlines attached to them. Otherwise, what you call "goals" are really only pipe dreams, and you'll never move yourself toward your financial dreams.

Look at Which Expenses You're Willing to Cut

If you haven't yet looked at all of your expenses and decided which are priority items that you want to keep in your budget, do so now. Come back here when you're done.

Know Your Income

Before you can establish a budget, you have to know exactly how much money you have coming in every month from your employer, after taxes, union dues, medical insurance, 401(k) contributions, and so on. You must track all this information. If you haven't already done this, go back to it; then come back to this section, to work on your budget.

Getting Started

To make your first stab at a budget, simply fill out WORKSHEET 4-1.

YOUR FIRST BUDGET

Monthly income		$
Monthly obligations	−	$
Monthly amount needed for the goals	−	$
Balance	=	$
Checking the balance		$

If the balance in WORKSHEET 4-1 is a positive number, you're done! You've established a budget for yourself that, while perhaps not easy to stick to, will certainly be doable.

If, however, the balance is a negative number, you have an unbalanced budget and need to look again at your goals, expenses, and income. (You may want to use a pencil for the worksheets in the two following sections in case you have to revise them again, and again, and again!)

Revisit Your Goals

Goal	Date	Amount needed	Priority 1-5	Monthly amount
		$		$
		$		$
		$		$
		$		$
		$		$
		$		$
		$		$

Now is the time to go back through your goals and rework them, if you can. Wherever possible, change the amount of time or money needed, starting with your lowest-priority items. WORKSHEET 4-2 can help.

Take a Harder Look at Your Expenses

Another way to balance your budget is to look more closely at your expenses. This will help you think through expenses you can cut further, and there are concrete suggestions for ways to cut back on your spending later in this book.

Decide Whether You Can Increase Your Income

A final way to balance your budget is to find ways to increase your income and find more money. Be sure, however, that these opportunities for added income are actually in the bag; don't count on "possible" income when budgeting.

Take a Second Stab at a Budget

With revised goals and a new spending plan, you're ready for version two of your budget. See WORKSHEET 4-3.

WORKSHEET 4-3
VERSION TWO OF YOUR BUDGET

Monthly income		$
Monthly financial obligations	_	$
Monthly amount needed for your needs	_	$
Balance	=	$

Checking the Balance—Again

If your balance is now positive, you're done! Congratulations on working through your first budget. Chances are, though, that it's still negative, and you'll have to continue this process through many renditions. Start again: Revisit your goals, look at your expenses, and decide whether you can increase your income.

Don't get discouraged by all this revising—this is the essence of budgeting. If the process were easy—that is, if you could come up with a workable budget on your first try—people wouldn't have trouble living with budgets.

Continue This Process Until You Have a Budget

This process will give you another chance to work on a budget but do this one in pencil because you'll probably need to work through the numbers again. Keep going until the budget is completely balanced, and once you're able to live with. The keywords in this section are "able to live with." Never forget that you are going to live with this budget every hour of every day until the day you meet your financial goals. If you don't think you can do that, revise your budget again!

CHAPTER 5

FREEZE YOUR SPENDING FOR THE SHORT TERM

If your spending is getting the best of you, creating more and more debt for your family, try freezing your spending for the next several months. Freezing your spending isn't easy, but it can stop your accelerating debt dead in its tracks.

What Freezing Really Means

Freezing means going cold turkey on your spending—you temporarily stop buying. For the short term, you cut out all but an essential spending. Your cuts will include clothing, shoes, movies, eBooks, apps, small and large appliances, decorative items, linens, phone and computer accessories, and so on. You decide to freeze your spending for a predetermined amount of time—usually six to twelve months—and then just stop shopping. Of course, you can still buy groceries and the required supplies for your home, but you don't buy anything else.

Some people believe that they must spend in order to keep the American economy going. While consumer spending does impact how much money many businesses make, your six or nine months of thriftiness is not going to spin the economy into an uncontrolled recession.

Reduce Temptation During a Freeze

People who temporarily freeze spending usually find that the best way to stay the course is to steer clear of opportunities to spend money:

- Don't visit websites of your favorite stores.
- Steer clear of eBay, Etsy, Kickstarter, and the like. Some of the items on those sites are unique enough that you may feel you must buy them in order to get a once-in-a-lifetime opportunity.
- If invited to an in-home party (such as CAbi, Pampered Chef, Mary Kay), politely refuse. There will be other such parties when you're not on a spending freeze.
- Don't stop at outlet malls when you travel.
- Unsubscribe from e-mails from your favorite stores and sites.
- Don't go to the shopping-mall food court for a quick meal.
- Don't meet friends for an afternoon at the mall or any other store.
- If you're playing golf, taking a yoga class, or doing any similar activity, don't go into the clubhouse, showroom, or gift shop.

- Don't go window-shopping. It generally doesn't work, and temptation gets the best of you.
- When grocery shopping, don't inadvertently wander into the consumer-goods section of the store.
- Send gift cards or money instead of actual purchases as gifts, so that you don't have to go to a store or browse a site.

The following sections will help you freeze your spending a little less painfully.

Establish What's Really a Need

Understanding the difference between a need and a want is really the crux of sorting out your finances. In an effort to make ourselves feel better about being consumers, we often elevate wants to the level of needs. However, needs are generally few, at least in the realm of products that you can buy:

- Shelter
- Clothing
- Food and water

Thousands of years ago, this list meant a mud, straw, or wooden hut, along with some animal skins, and just enough calories to survive. Today, these basic human needs have become so intertwined with wants that we're not sure how to separate them. Yes, you need shelter, but you don't need a four-bedroom open-concept home, a three-car garage, a kitchen with cherry cabinets, and a bonus room over the garage. That's a want.

The same applies for clothing. Humans need a way to stay warm and dry, but we don't need fifteen suits or ten pairs of jeans. Those are wants. While everyone needs food and water to survive, that food does not have to come from a five-star restaurant, or for that matter, from any sort of restaurant at all. Preparing your meals at home will fill the bill just fine.

The desire to own and consume is very strong, and it often seems to justify nearly any purchase in the name of needs. Don't buy into it. Instead, use WORKSHEET 5-1 to list your every need (you might want to use a pencil, though, and keep a good eraser handy). Be very specific on your list: Don't just list "house"; instead, write a description of the house you need and the amount it will cost.

Also consider the consequence of not making each purchase by asking yourself the following questions:

- Would you or others around you die?
- Would you or others suffer physical pain or extreme physical discomfort?
- Would your health or the health of others suffer in the long term?
- Do you know for sure that you would lose your job or home without this item?

If none of these would happen, it likely isn't a need; it's a want, and you have no business buying it during a spending freeze. In general, the best way to tell the difference between wants and needs is that the consequence of not purchasing a needed item is grave, while the consequence of not buying a wanted item is trivial.

Suppose, for example; you decide that decorating your house for every season is a need, not a want. Now consider the consequence of not decorating for every season. Will you or your family suffer somehow? Truly? You may have convinced yourself that it's unthinkable to not decorate for Halloween and that it won't cost that much anyway, but you're in a spending freeze, which means no spending on anything but a need.

WORKSHEET 5-1
NEEDS VERSUS WANTS

Need(description)	Amount	Consequence of not buying
	$	
	$	
	$	
	$	

Establish—and Stick to—a Shopping List for Your Needs

Before you leave the house and head out to spend money, write out a shopping list of your needs (which are likely to include only groceries and toiletries). Be sure that they're needs, and don't pad the list because you're in the mood to buy. Keep in mind that you are probably feeling deprived, so you may try to satisfy your spending itch by splurging on groceries and toiletries.

Before you leave the store, write down everything you need to get, and also scribble in an estimate of how much each item will cost. Then total the bill. If it's less than you planned to spend, stop writing out your list and immediately go to the store. If the total is more than you planned to spend, begin crossing items off your list before you go until you get down to the budgeted amount.

Don't justify veering from the list because something is "such a good deal." Instead, remember that the best possible deal is to spend $0, so even if an item is a half price, you can't buy it unless it's on your list.

Then, buy only the items on the list. Don't add items to the list and then cross them off while you're standing in the checkout lane. Instead, stick absolutely to your list. If you see something, you're sure you need, but it isn't on your list, put it on next week's list when you get home. Today, you can buy only what's on your list. Be vigilant about this process, and you'll never overspend on groceries and toiletries again.

Try to Get the Best Deals on Your Needs

You're in a spending freeze for a reason, so make every penny count by shopping for deals on your needs. Say your shampoo costs $8 per bottle at the superstore. But you find an online coupon for 25 percent off an online drugstore, with free shipping. The shampoo costs $9 per bottle online, but with the discount, it's only $6.75, a better deal. Try this with everything you buy locally, just to be sure you're getting the best deal. Yes, shopping locally is a better bet for your community, but in a spending freeze, all bets are off, and you're trying to get the most bang for your buck.

Before you buy anything online or go into any store, type the name of the store and the word "coupon" into your search engine. Make this a habit: Don't check out online or head to a store without checking for discounts. You can also find coupon apps on your smartphone!

One caveat: If the online deal requires you to spend more than you want to in order to get free shipping, or if shipping costs make an item more expensive than you would pay locally, forget it. You'll be better off at your local store.

Put Away Your Credit Cards

Seriously, put them away for at least six months. Put them in a safe place that's hard to get to, such as a safe-deposit box at the bank (which will probably cost around $30 per year, an amount that's worth spending if it keeps you from getting further into debt). The farther away the credit cards are from you, the better. You'll also need to delete any saved credit card information online since you'll still be able to buy without having the card in front of you.

Then, for six months, pay for all of your day-to-day purchases with cash and pay your bills with a check or electronic bill-pay. When you're shopping for purchases that are allowed—such as groceries and toiletries—write out a list before you go, estimate how much you'll need, and take no more than $10 over that amount.

When you're not supposed to be making any purchases, limit the amount of cash you carry around to $5 and a few quarters. That will allow you to pay for parking if you need to, but not lunch . . . or a flat-screen TV.

Tuck-Away Your Debit Card

Although a debit card is technically like cash or a check, in reality, it feels much more like a credit card. Because you don't hand over cash, you may feel as though you're not really paying for this purchase, much like when you use a credit card.

And if those funds are earmarked for other needs (like paying off your debt or saving for a vacation), you'll end up without enough money to meet your needs by the end of the month.

If you take $80 in cash to the grocery store, you'll be very careful not to exceed that amount and be stuck at the register. But if you take a debit card, you're not likely to be nearly as careful. Put the debit card in the same place you put the credit cards—your best bet is in a safe-deposit box.

Create a Wish List

A wish list is an outlet for your hot little fingers and creative mind while you're in a spending freeze. The basic idea is that you write down everything you'd ever like to buy. The list may range from a new TV to teeth-whitening strips to a sailboat. Anything you're not allowed to buy during a spending freeze is fair game, and nothing on the list has to be sensible or practical or a wise financial decision.

Sometimes when you're not spending, you feel disconnected from our consumer-oriented society, and a wish list makes you feel like your old self again. When you feel the itch to spend, go online or look at a friend's catalogs. Write down the item number, description, page number, and so on of any item that looks interesting.

Act as if you're really going to buy the item, but don't. Just add the item to your list, and let the list sit for a while. The act of writing the item down or putting it into an online cart will feel, strangely enough, very similar to how you feel when you actually buy something. It sounds crazy, but it works!

When you brainstorm your wish list, think pie-in-the-sky. You're just day-dreaming right now—later, you can make your list more realistic. So write down whatever you can imagine in your future. But make sure it's your wish list. Don't put a sailboat on your list if you really don't like water!

Just listing the items can be cathartic when you want to buy, buy, buy. But listing the items on WORKSHEET 5-2 can also help you cross some items off. When you write down an item's name and cost, also check off one of the three needs categories: "Need Today," "Need This Month," or "Would Like Someday." If none applies, don't check anything off. Tomorrow, revisit any item that you indicated you needed today. Is the need still strong? In a month, review any items that you needed this month, and also look at the items that you'd like someday. Do you still feel strongly about them? Cross off any item you no longer feel you need and/or check off new categories for some items.

Worksheet 5-2

Item name	Cost	Need today	Need this month	Would like some-day
	$			
	$			
	$			
	$			
	$			

By doing so, you've narrowed your list to items you would clearly like to own and can begin to save for when your spending freeze is over. You also have a ready-made list if anyone asks you what you really want for your birthday.

CHAPTER 6

CUT YOUR EXPENSES AT HOME

If you're having trouble putting together a balanced budget, here are some solid ideas for cutting your expenses at home right now. Each one by itself may not save you tons of money, but if you combine several of them, the savings will add up over time.

Turn the Thermostat Down (or Up)

A simple way to cut your heating and cooling costs is to turn your thermostat down one degree in winter and up one degree in summer. One degree—which you probably won't even notice—can save you up to a hundred dollars a year on your heating and cooling bills.

Using a programmable thermostat is a simple way to do this. These thermostats automatically turn your temperatures up and down at preset times. So if you are always in bed by 11:00 P.M. in the winter, you program the thermostat to turn down the heat at 11:15 P.M., saving you money all night. It then turns the temperature back up at 6:30 A.M. so you wake up to a toasty house. It turns the temperature down again while you're away at work and turns it up just before you get home.

These thermostats are easy to program—look for one that offers daytime and nighttime settings, plus separate settings for the weekend, when you're likely to be home more and sleep in later. Because programmable thermostats actually turn the temperature down, they pay for themselves in a couple of months.

Programmable thermostats are available at all home-improvement stores and cost between $35 and $75, depending on the features they offer. Look for one that has both weekday and weekend settings, especially if you tend to wake up later in the morning on Saturdays and Sundays.

Get Your Books and Movies from the Library

Here's an important budgeting fact: Your local library lets you borrow stuff for free! From print books and eBooks to audiobooks and movies, your library has a wide range of free opportunities to entertain you and your family. Library cards are also free, and if you're looking for digital media (like eBooks, audiobooks, and movies), you can do your borrowing from home. Take advantage of online holds, too, which let you direct the next available copy of any item to you, at whichever branch you choose. With hardcover books averaging $26, paperbacks at around $15, and eBooks at $10, checking books out of your library can save you a bundle. The same goes for movies and audiobooks.

Whatever you do, don't return your books and movies late! The point here is to save money, not spend it. Although fines on books are often just 25 or 50 cents per day, that's per book, so if you have more than one, you'll pay more.

Fines on movies can run $2–$3 per day, each. If you're not careful, you can end up owing the library $23—wait, that's my story, not yours!

Cut Cable and Phone Cords

Although you may think that cable TV is part of life's necessities, it's an extra service that you should subscribe to only if you have plenty of extra money each month—after you pay all of your other financial obligations. Cord cutting is a big trend right now, as people order cable Internet without the TV and phone bundles.

How does this work? Well, first you have to live in a cable area that has a reasonably priced Internet-only service. I got lucky after a recent move and was able to get super-fast cable Internet for $41 per month. The next closest price point was $59 per month, for much slower cable and some basic TV channels, a savings of over $200 per year.

Cord cutters get most of their news via the Internet, and watch shows through Netflix, Hulu Plus, Amazon Prime, and other providers, or directly from each show's website if episodes are offered. In general, this means watching shows later—and in some cases, much later, like months or years—than cable TV viewers are watching those shows. And some web-only customers aren't able to get any channels at all on their TVs, even the free network stations, without purchasing an antenna, which can eat up much of your savings.

The greatest benefit may not be financial, however, but a substantial windfall of time. After cutting the cord, some people run back to cable TV. But many find that they read more and are more active than they were when they had 50—or 500—channels at their disposal.

Also, if you still have a landline and find that you're not using it much, consider giving it the boot, too. However, if getting rid of your landline will increase your need for cell minutes (and you will pay a higher fee for that), double-check your math. Find out what other cell companies are offering their customers, such as free incoming calls, free nights and weekends, nighttime rates starting earlier than 9:00 P.M., free calls to customers on the same network, free text messaging, and so on.

When your contract is up, if you can switch to another cell company and save money by not having a landline, go for it.

Shop Around for Car Insurance

Car insurance rates vary so widely that you're doing yourself a disservice by not checking around. I've had prices vary as much as $800 per year, with no discernible difference in coverage. So, once a year, do a quick search online of insurance rates for your car and driving record (many sites will give you an instant quote). If you find a substantially lower rate, ask your current agent to requote your policy, to see whether he or she can match what you've found.

Speeding, reckless driving, and driving under the influence can ruin your finances. Not only will you get socked with the soaring cost of tickets, but your insurance rates could double or triple.

Use WORKSHEET 6-1 as a handy place to compare rates and coverage.

WORKSHEET 6-1
INSURANCE COMPARISONS

Insurance company	Semiannual premiums	Type of coverage
	$	
	$	
	$	
	$	
	$	

If your insurance payments are still uncomfortably high after you shop around, try raising your deductibles (the amount you pay out of pocket if you have an accident, your car is stolen, or a flood washes your car away). You can save quite a bit on your annual insurance costs by increasing your deductibles from $250 to $500 or from $500 to $1,000 (per incident). Some companies don't offer high deductibles, but if yours does, see how much of a difference raising it can make. Do be sure, though, to put the amount of your deductible in a savings account, so that you have the money if you need to repair your car.

Avoid Extended Warranties

No matter what major purchase you make—car, furnace, computer, or dishwasher—you'll probably be offered an extended warranty by the company selling you the product. For "just" $129 or $59, you can add an extra year to the existing warranty. Sometimes you can even add three or four years of protection. These extended warranties can be a good investment in some cases, but they're a bad idea at other times.

When Not to Buy an Extended Warranty

If the product you're purchasing has any of the following characteristics, steer clear of an extended warranty:

- You intend to own the product for only as long as the original warranty is in effect.
- Within a few years, the product will be out of date, and you'll want or need to get a better, more powerful model.
- The purchase price is low enough that you wouldn't be strapped if you had to buy another in a few years.
- Repairing this product is simple and inexpensive.
- The cost of this product is likely to decrease over the next few years. This is true of many electronics products, and especially TVs.
- The extended warranty costs more than 20 percent of the purchase price.

When to Buy an Extended Warranty

Do get an extended warranty if any of the following is true for you:

- This piece of equipment is critical to your livelihood.
- You know you can't afford to replace the product if it breaks.
- The warranty is very inexpensive.

Check out the insurance company before you buy an extended warranty. Look into how long it has been in business (check its website) and search the Better Business Bureau's database (www.bbb.org) to get a sense of whether this company will even be in business in three years.

You can set up your own "extended warranty" savings account. If the product you're buying costs $120 and comes with a one-year warranty, put $10 per month into your savings account. When the year is up, you'll have enough money in savings to cover the purchase of a new product, should the old one break. If the replacement cost of the product tends to go up over time, as is the case with cars, put a little more than the existing cost into your savings account.

Buy Reliable, High-Quality Products

This idea may seem to go against most money-saving advice, but the truth is that high-quality products tend to last longer. If you buy a well-researched, reliable car instead of an inexpensive economy car, you'll pay substantially more. But if the economy car fizzles in three years and the higher-quality car keeps running for fifteen years after that, you'll save money in the long run.

Keep the following tips in mind, however, when shopping for quality:

- If buying the quality item will wreck your budget, either save up and come back when you can afford it, or make do with the less expensive item.
- Don't automatically assume that higher price equals higher quality. Sometimes, higher prices are simply the result of savvy businesspeople thinking that consumers will associate their products with quality if they charge a lot.
- Read online reviews of the product. Amazon (www.amazon.com) tends to have the largest number of reviews for products. Read through them and be sure you're getting the highly rated product you're paying for.
- Don't worry about buying a quality product if you're not planning to keep it very long. If you're on vacation and forget your swimsuit, don't spend a lot for another one—just buy something that will get you through the week.
- You can get high-quality, albeit used, items for a fraction of their original cost by shopping online auctions and consignment shops. See the following section for details.

Don't Buy Trendy Items

Before you buy anything, ask yourself whether you're buying it because it's the best-quality item you can get for the price or because it's a popular item that makes you feel good for the moment. Women's shoes and purses come to mind as short-term, trendy items that tend to be out of style in a year or two, but not always. If you intend to keep shoes, boots, or purses for many years, avoid colors and styles that will look dated in a year or two.

Many budgets are blown on novelty items, and what's so frustrating about buying them is that a couple of weeks or months later, you can't figure out what you saw in the item in the first place! Before you buy anything, apply the one-year test: Is this an item you'll want a year from now? If not, pass it up.

Become a Late Adopter

You don't have to be the first kid on your block to get the cool stuff. Personal electronics, especially, tend to have a high initial price and then settle into a lower price for late adopters. For example, big-screen TVs and smartphones come way down in price within a year of their debut. So wait a bit, and then make your purchase—if you've budgeted for the item.

Shop Online Auctions, Tag Sales, and Resale Shops

Whether you're furnishing a nursery or building a wardrobe, online auctions, tag sales (also called garage sales or yard sales), and resale or consignment shops, including those from Goodwill Industries and the Salvation Army, can save you a bundle.

Does this go against the advice in the preceding section to buy high-quality items? Not necessarily. Just because an item is being sold in an auction or at a tag sale or resale shop doesn't mean it isn't a high-quality item. The mere fact that the item has lasted long enough to be worn by someone until it no longer fit or the person became bored with it points to the fact that this is a long-lasting product.

Cheaply made products don't usually end up on auctions or at tag sales and resale shops—instead, they get thrown out. Some low-quality items do appear, however, so you need to know a couple of tricks for shopping at tag sales and resale shops. These techniques are discussed in the following sections.

Win at Auctions

If there's an item you've been looking for but can't quite afford, get yourself over to an online auction site such as eBay (www.ebay.com) to see whether anyone is offering it at less-than-retail value. And don't just go once: If you don't see what you're looking for, go back every week or so, since millions of items are listed every week.

You can search for items by keywords (better than browsing, which is too tempting), and you may be given two options: an option to submit a bid and compete with other interested buyers, and an option to buy it immediately at a higher price.

You may also be given the option to make an offer, which means the seller wants to hear what you think the item is worth. Be sure to check what the shipping and handling charges will be, as those costs can add up.

If you decide to bid on an item, you'll utilize an automatic bidding function that will keep electronically raising your bid until you reach your highest price. Just be very firm about what your highest price is, and don't be tempted to go above it, get caught up in a bidding euphoria, and blow your budget. If you're afraid you'll be tempted to bid higher than the limit you originally set, stay away from e-mail in the final minutes before the auction expires.

Online auctions like eBay are also a great place to sell your unused items. But beware that you'll put a lot of time into photographing, describing, answering questions about, boxing up, and shipping your items, and eBay also takes a chunk of your earnings as a fee. Selling on eBay isn't free, but it can be a way to free up some cash in your budget.

Prepare a Shopping List Ahead of Time

If you go to a tag sale or consignment shop to browse, you're likely to end up buying something that you don't need, and even the deepest discount isn't a bargain if you don't need the item. Before you leave home, determine your needs and put them down on paper—and then don't buy anything that's not on your list, no matter how wonderful or how cheap it is.

Purchase High-Quality, Undamaged Products

If you're interested in an item, pick it up and carry it with you. If you're not sure you want it and don't pick it up, it's liable to be gone when you go back to look for it, especially at a tag sale. At-large resale shops like Goodwill Industries and the Salvation Army, you may never again find that blue shirt among the hundreds of blue shirts they stock.

After you've browsed the store (online or brick and mortar), turn to the items you have in your cart or are watching online. Look closely at any product before buying it, including enlarging online photos so that you can see details. Examine it for damage of any sort; turn it over and inside out to see whether it's cheaply made or is something that will last a while. Keep in mind that even buying a $2 chair or a $1 pair of pants isn't a good deal if it breaks or rips the first time you use it.

Many resale shops have discount days—say, 10 percent off on Wednesday mornings. If there's an item you're looking for, find out in advance when sale days are.

Consider Haggling—or Not

A lot of people haggle at tag sales. Most people holding the sales expect it, but the choice is up to you. You may save a few bucks, but the person having the garage sale is also trying to make some money, so if the marked price seems acceptable to you, pay it.

Reduce Gift Expenditures

Contrary to popular belief, you don't have to purchase gifts for your friends, family, and coworkers on every birthday, anniversary, or Hallmark holiday. You can, for example, save money on holiday gifts by drawing names among your friends, family, and/or coworkers. For any occasion, you can give a small donation to a favorite charity in the name of the gift recipient and send a card explaining the gift. Consider making gifts as well: cookies, bread, soups, and so on. Also, anyone—from a close friend to a casual acquaintance to a family member you don't see often—will appreciate a simple, handwritten note from you.

One way to save on gifts is not to give them at all! Let friends, family, and coworkers know that while you're getting your finances under control, you won't be giving—and don't expect to get—presents for the next few years. If you've been in the habit of exchanging holiday gifts, send a note to this effect in late September or early October to give people time to adjust.

Avoid Dry-Cleaning

Unless the product you're cleaning absolutely, positively has to be dry-cleaned (check the label), don't use this expensive service. Many articles of clothing—even wool, cashmere, linen, and many silks—can be hand-washed or washed using the delicate cycle of your washer, using an extra-mild detergent. It's estimated that more than half of all clothes that say "dry-clean only" can be machine-washed, so think of all the money you can save.

What if I must dry-clean an item I own?

If you do need to dry-clean a product, be sure to go online to check for coupons. You may be able to get from 10 to 30 percent off at your local dry-cleaners.

You may also be able to "dry-clean" your items yourself, using an at-home kit. Dryel, Woolite, Bounce, and others make low-cost home dry-cleaning kits that work in your dryer. You put your item into the provided bag, spot-cleaning beforehand as necessary, and run it through the dryer cycle. Voilà!

Use professional dry-cleaning services for suede, leather, and any items that would be difficult to iron. But keep in mind the next time you shop for clothes that dry-clean-only items cost you more in the long run.

Take Cheaper Vacations

Advertising may lead you to believe that the only way you can be a good spouse or parent is to take your family on a cruise, to Disney World, or to sunny vacation spots in the winter. Remember the source, though: These ads come from places that need you to visit for them to make money.

If you plan to take a vacation this year, be sure to estimate the taxes on hotel rooms, rental cars, and meals. In some areas, these taxes can total nearly 20 percent.

The truth is, though, that for a vacation to be great, all you need to do is get out of your current environment for a while and do something fun and, perhaps, different. To save money on your vacation, for example, you can stay right in your own state, perhaps in an area, you've never visited before. Use Kayak (www.kayak.com) to compare rates and find your best deal on an extended-stay hotel, which will usually have a kitchenette so you can cook your own meals and offers discounts for stays of seven nights or more. If you already own camping equipment, consider going that route. Pack picnic lunches and look for free or low-cost attractions, such as museums, parks, zoos, and so on. Hiking is nearly always free and is a great way to find new adventures.

Before booking your vacation spot, read reviews from your fellow consumers about their experiences. A lot of "it was gross" comments won't make even the lowest price worthwhile, while a bargain-priced motel with a lot of "it was lovely" comments is a deal to snag.

Remember that just because you're on vacation, you don't have a license to spend money that you would never dream of spending at home.

To keep shopping extravaganzas to a limit, consider bringing a check card (a debit card, but with a cap) for all your vacation expenses, including hotel, rental cars, and so on. Instead of putting your vacation on a credit card, use your check card, which some banks offer free or at a reduced rate. You'll get nervous as you see the balance dwindle and won't be tempted to buy souvenirs or other unplanned items.

CHAPTER 7

REDUCE YOUR BIGGEST EXPENSES

If your financial obligations exceed your income by so much that creating a budget seems impossible right now, take steps to cut your biggest expenses over the next few months and years. These are not easy cuts to make, but they can help you get back on solid financial footing.

Move to a Smaller House or Apartment

Real-estate agents, mortgage lenders, and apartment brokers can be awfully generous with your money. When you go house hunting, they'll tell you that you can afford a lot of house or apartment—it's in their best interest to do so. Real-estate agents are paid a percentage of the price of the house you buy, mortgage lenders earn their money on fees and interest that rise with the purchase price of your home, and apartment brokers earn one or two months' rent.

But these parties don't have any interest in helping you manage your money over the long haul. Even mortgage lenders care only about whether you'll repay the loan on time, not whether you can barely make ends meet or are getting yourself deeper into credit card debt each year.

Real-estate agents and mortgage lenders aren't the only people who influence you to want to live in a big, expensive house. Advertising, movies, TV shows, and other forms of media send a clear message that the bigger and more expensive your house, the more you should be respected in this world.

Worried that you won't be able to fit all your stuff into a smaller house? Just accept that you won't fit it all in. Hold a tag sale, auction items off on eBay, or sell them on Craigslist, and you'll get rid of your extra items and generate some cash.

Want to get on solid financial footing? Forget what society and your friends, family, and coworkers say about big spaces. Instead, set out to find the smallest home in the best neighborhood with the best schools.

Home prices and rentals are usually based on square footage, quality, and location—location often being the most important. (This is why tiny, fixer-upper, ocean-view houses can cost ten or twenty times more than similar houses inland.) You don't want to skimp on quality and location; instead, the trick is to reduce your square footage.

You can probably live in half the square footage you're living in now if you pare down some of your belongings and live more efficiently. So aim for this: If you're living in 2,500 square feet, look at places that are 1,200 or 1,300 square feet. If you find this is just too cramped for your family, move up 100–300 square feet, but not much more than that, since your new place has to be substantially cheaper to make a move worthwhile .

You'll have expenses associated with moving, but if you move to a home that saves you enough money each month, those expenses will be worthwhile. (And if credit card debt is crushing you, you may also be able to pay off those credit cards at the same time.) This will help you work through some of the costs of staying versus moving.

Try to finance your new mortgage for the same number of years (or very close) that you have left on your current mortgage. Sure, your monthly payments will be lower if you increase the life of your loan, but you'll weaken your financial future in the process.

Keep in mind that if you're in a poor financial situation, mortgage lenders may not approve you for a loan right now, and a landlord may not approve your lease application. Before you put your current house up for sale or tell your landlord you're moving, get preapproved for a mortgage. You don't want to sell your house, and then find that you aren't in a position to get another mortgage at this time.

Buy a House Instead of Renting

If you're currently paying a hefty monthly rent on your house or apartment, consider buying a house. Keep in mind that buying a house isn't always a good idea—in fact when you're strapped for money and/or in debt, it may be a terrible idea. You may have trouble qualifying for a mortgage, and you might end up paying more (in the short term) for a house in property taxes, home-owner's insurance, maintenance, and repairs.

Assuming you can qualify for a mortgage (and it's always a good idea to get preapproved by a lender—a process that usually costs $30 or less) and have twenty or more years left on your mortgage, consider the following two situations that make financial sense when you're thinking of buying a house:

- You can mortgage a house that has some repair and mainte-nance issues on a fifteen-year loan for 60 percent (or less) of what you pay now.
- You can mortgage a move-in-ready house for fifteen years for the same as you're paying now.

In the first situation, you'll see an immediate improvement in your financial situation, but down the road, you may incur maintenance and repair costs that can add up. In the second situation, you won't see much of a change in your immediate financial picture, but you'll reap major benefits in the future.

Why the emphasis on fifteen-year loans? Because so much more of your payment goes toward principal (instead of interest) with a fifteen-year loan so that you can build a substantial amount of equity in your home in just five years. With a fifteen year loan, you'll pay off over 23 percent of your debt in the first five years. With a thirty-year loan, you'll pay off just under 6 percent in those same five years.

Why do experts think having a mortgage is a good type of debt?

Because, in spite of dips now and then, the price of houses tends to appreciate (go up) with time, so when people sell their homes, they can pay off the debt on the house and still have plenty of money left over. Also, you get a tax break on the interest you pay on your mortgage.

Rent Instead of Buying

Wait—doesn't this section say just the opposite of everything the last section touched? It does, but owning a house isn't for everyone—nor is it always the most economical way to go. Consider the following scenarios:

- You like where you live. Unless you're itching to move from your rental, stay put. Buying a home is a commitment of time as well as money, and if you're not feeling the urge to make that commitment right now, go with your gut.

  Don't listen to anyone who tells you that you "have to invest in the market right now" or "interest rates are going to skyrocket" or "you'll never get another chance like this." You have to be ready, and if you're not, keep on renting.

- You're planning to move in the next few years. If you're planning to live in an area for three years or fewer, you won't see enough appreciation on your house to make buying worthwhile.

  Instead, look for a rental that maximizes your budget while minimizing your square footage. And if you don't like the condition of rentals in your area, remember that you can do low-cost cosmetic work, like covering your older appliances with stainless-steel kits, painting walls, and floors, and making windows seem larger with beautiful curtains you buy on sale or make at home.

- Real-estate costs are astronomical in your area. Millions of New York City residents rent for life, especially if they can snag a rent-stabilized apartment. Between the cost of real estate ($500,000 for a 400-square-foot studio), the large down payment needed (which can run 25 percent, if a co-op board requires it), and high monthly maintenance fees (often upward of $1,000 per month), buying is impossible. If you're in a high-cost area like that, WORKSHEET 8-2 is likely going to show that buying isn't a good financial decision for you.

- You don't have the required down payment. Twenty percent is standard these days. If you don't have it, don't borrow from family or your 401(k) to buy, because you'll just put pressure on your financial picture and risk going into debt. Instead, keep saving (and renting) until you do.

Rethink Your Ideas about Transportation

Cars can cost a lot of money: Payments or leases usually run several hundred dollars a month; maintenance and repairs are expensive; over-the-top gasoline prices can squeeze your budget, and registration and insurance can set you back more than a thousand dollars per year.

Look Into Public Transportation

If you live in an area where you can walk or bike to work and the grocery store, or if you have a reliable mass-transit system in your area, consider getting rid of your car.

Many people wonder how you'll get home for the holidays or take vacations if you don't have a car. The simplest solution is to rent a car when you need one. You may pay a lot for the rental five or six times a year, but that cost won't come close to the amount you now pay in car payments, insurance, maintenance, and so on.

To most people, this is a revolutionary—if not repulsive—idea. Having a car is like having a name: Everybody has one! Well, they don't. Plenty of people who live in large cities don't own cars, and they love it. And more and more eco-conscious folks are touting the benefits of walking or biking or riding public transportation to work, so you're not completely alone there, either.

Even if you're not a city dweller or staunch friend of the earth, getting rid of your car can make sense. There's an immediate financial impact: If you're making monthly car payments, those will stop right away. And if your car is paid off, you'll get some cash that will help you pay your other bills.

Go the Bicycle or Moped Route

Even if public transportation in your area isn't up to par, you may still be able to live without a car, especially if you live in an area with a mild climate. Cycling to work every day gives you two immediate benefits: 1) It saves you money, and 2) it gets you into shape. Many companies now offer a shower at work, so if you get sweaty on the ride in, you can wash up and change into work clothes when you get there. By installing a pack on your bike (called panniers or townies) that holds two sacks of groceries, you can also stop by the store on your way home.

If being completely reliant on your physical prowess to get you around town is a little much for you, consider investing in a moped. These economical vehicles are like low-powered motorcycles and generally run from $1,200 (used) to about $2,500 (gleaming and new). If you can sell your car and buy a moped, saving bundles in gas, insurance, and registration might make getting a little wind-blown not seem so bad. Plus, mopeds are way cool.

Keep a Paid-Off, Reliable Car

If you have a reliable car that's paid off, runs well, and costs a reasonable amount in gasoline, maintenance, and insurance, you're probably better off not selling it. A car like this is just too rare to part with.

Another situation in which selling your car isn't a good idea is if you're upside down on your loan—meaning your car is worth less than you owe on it. If you're upside down on your loan and interest rates are lower than they were when you bought the car, look into refinancing your car loan.

Next time you buy a car, purchase the highest-quality model you can afford, put as much money down on it as you can, and arrange for the fewest number of payments possible. Then plan to drive the car—payment-free—for as many years as you can after you pay it off.

Big or Small?

If you're in the market for a car, you'll need to make some important decisions. Do you want a Chevrolet Suburban or a Smart Car? Do you want a minivan or a Mini Cooper? Do you want a Hummer or a Fiat? Another way to put this is, are you going to go with a roomy interior and low mpg, or a small interior and high mpg?

Small cars offer a few financial advantages:

- They cost less. Sure, you can get a souped-up small car, but if you stay conservative, you're going to spend less on a small car than on a larger car with the same options. If you finance your car, this means that your monthly payments will be lower or you'll be able to finance your car for fewer months.
- They often get better mileage. Given high gas prices, better mileage can have substantial financial ramifications on your

budget. Remember, however, that not all small cars are fuel-efficient. You may opt for a slightly larger hybrid, which will cost you more than a small car but will save you plenty of gasoline over the years. Do your homework, and then do the math.

- Your auto insurance may be cheaper. This didn't use to be the case, as smaller cars were also often less safe, so insurance for smaller cars wasn't any less than for larger ones. But today's small cars often do just as well in crash tests as larger, more expensive cars, and because the smaller cars cost less to replace and do less damage to other vehicles, insurance companies charge less in premiums.

- You can park in all those parking-garage spaces that say "compact cars only." Finding parking for a smaller car is always easier.

Choose Between Leasing and Buying

Except for a few business-related tax breaks, leasing a car will never improve your financial picture. Leasing a car amounts to borrowing it for a specified number of months or years and, at the end of your contract, giving it back. Leasing is attractive to many people because your monthly payments are substantially lower than when you buy and the length of a lease contract is usually fairly short, which means you can get a new car more often than if you buy. But leasing is really just having a long-term rental car.

If you must own a car, don't lease! Instead, buy a reliable car on the fewest number of payments you can afford and plan to drive it for six, eight, or ten years. After you've paid it off, keep making the payments to your savings account so that you can pay cash for your next car.

To improve your financial picture, stop thinking of a car as an extension of who you are. Ultimately, if you're miserable because you're sinking deeper and deeper into debt and/or don't know how you're going to pay your bills this month, who cares what you're driving? You also want to stop thinking of a car payment as a fact of life. Just imagine how much more breathing room you'd have each month if you didn't have a car payment. Well, leasing never lets you go there. You're locked into making a payment every month, and when you're done paying, you still don't own a car. You just have to go out and get another one and make the lease payments on it for several more years.

Change Jobs

Getting a different job can have a variety of immediate impacts, each discussed in the following sections.

A New Job Can Increase Your Paycheck

A job is always more than just a paycheck. Depending on the job you have, it can be an opportunity to test yourself, develop new skills, meet all sorts of new people, travel, express yourself, see your values turned into action, and so on. When your financial situation is bleak, however, the paycheck can be the most important aspect of having a job. Whatever you do, don't take a job with no growth or one that is in direct opposition to your values just for the money—unless you can guarantee that the job is temporary. If you think you can make more money at another job, however, do begin your search immediately. Even if you end up turning down another job offer, knowing what other jobs pay—and what other companies expect from you—is worth the time spent searching.

Don't forget to look within your own company for a higher-paying job. Let your supervisor know that you're itching for more responsibility, and keep your eye on internal job postings. Take advantage of any training your company offers. In addition, find out what skills and training the job you have in mind calls for and see whether your company will pay for (or reimburse you for) classes at your local college or job-training site.

A New Job Can Reduce Your Commute

Reducing or eliminating your commute (which can happen if you find a job that lets you telecommute) means that you save gas and maintenance on your car. You may also, potentially, eliminate the need for a car altogether. Although many people commute more than an hour each way, commuting isn't free, and it can take a toll on your finances.

A New Job Can Reduce or Eliminate Your Insurance Costs

If you pay more for your medical, dental, and life insurance than you can afford, look for a job that offers these benefits free or subsidizes them. Even if the job pays a lower salary, your bottom line may improve by having these benefits paid for.

Note that you'll first need to locate the amount you pay every two weeks for insurance. If you pay for it on your own every month, divide that by 2.165. If you pay it semiannually, divide by 13; if you pay annually, divide by 26. If your employer takes it out of your paycheck every two weeks, use the amount shown on your pay stub.

You'll also need to know your gross income every two weeks on your current job and on the job you're considering. Gross income is the amount you're paid before taxes and deductions are taken out of your check. This is often stated as an hourly wage (say, $11.50 per hour) or as an annual salary ($23,000 per year). To find this amount, look on your pay stub for the amount listed as "gross income."

A New Job Can Reduce or Eliminate What You Pay for Child Care

Some companies offer free or subsidized daycare, either in the company's facility or at a daycare center close by. If child-care costs are putting pressure on your finances, seek out a company that offers this benefit.

Working Mother's annual listing of the best companies to work for includes child-care assistance as a criterion (www.working-mother.com/bestcompanies). As you're searching for a new job, use this list to find companies that offer the a typical benefit of on-site daycare.

Before jumping ship to take advantage of free or subsidized daycare, be sure that the company offers a comparable salary and good insurance plan for your family.

A New Job Can Reduce Your Need for an Expensive

Wardrobe Although this may seem like a silly benefit to consider when changing jobs, the costs of buying and caring for clothing can add up throughout the year. If you're able to find a job with a casual dress code, with clothes you already own and can wash in a washing machine, you can save money.

CHAPTER 8

RESTRUCTURE A HEAVY
DEBT BURDEN

If your debts are crushing you, you may need to take action to restructure them through some means: credit counseling, debt consolidation, or selling some of your assets. Here are some basics of debt restructuring.

How Debt Is Restructured

Does this situation sound like you? You have too much debt to handle—maybe you've charged more than you can afford on several credit cards, you have school loans plus a car and house payment, and the usual payments for utilities and food.

You're having trouble making monthly payments, perhaps you are already a few months behind, and you're starting to be (or have been for some time) hassled by debt collectors.

If so, debt restructuring is exactly what you need. The idea is that you change the way your debt is structured by lowering interest rates, lengthening repayment schedules, combining several payments into one smaller payment, or getting some of the debts forgiven, and at the same time, stop you from getting further into debt. You may have to give something up, but you'll probably come out way ahead in the long run.

If you've been using a check-cashing service to get cash for your paycheck (or a cash loan against your next paycheck), stop immediately. Most of these companies charge a ridiculous amount of money for their services. Instead, open a bank account (look for a totally free one), which you can open with anywhere from $5 to $50.

There are some ways to restructure your current debts. You might see a credit counselor to discuss your options (this is a good place to begin because it's usually free), consolidate most of your debts into one payment, sell some of your assets, use the equity in your house to pay off your debts, or declare bankruptcy.

Get Credit Counseling

Credit counseling is available from for-profit and nonprofit agencies, and each assigns you a counselor who reviews your debts, assets, and income to help you identify options other than bankruptcy. Sometimes credit counselors are bona fide financial gurus, but more often they're simply well-trained, well-meaning volunteers who offer an excellent service. All credit-counseling agencies offer their services in complete confidentiality and may offer services online or via phone, as well as face-to-face consultations.

Keep in mind, however, that not all credit-counseling agencies are nonprofit, and some are almost like scams.

Make Sure the Counseling Is Free

Your initial counseling session(s) should be completely free. If it isn't, get out as fast as you can! Many wonderful nonprofit credit-counseling agencies exist, so don't waste your money on an agency that charges you for counseling. While you may have to pay a small fee to consolidate your debt, the counseling session itself—in which your finances are sorted out, and advice is offered—should not require any fee.

Get Comfortable with Your Counselor

Be sure you trust your counselor and feel confident in his or her abilities. If you don't, find out whether another counselor can be assigned to you. Keep in mind, however, that your agency is probably a nonprofit organization with limited resources. You should have a darned good reason for wanting to be assigned a new counselor before you ask for this special treatment.

Take Advantage of Free Financial-Education Opportunities Many credit-counseling agencies also offer free short seminars, online videos, or downloadable brochures on how to get out of debt, manage money, save for a down payment on a house, save for retirement, and so on. If you're not ready to speak to a counselor but want more information, consider taking advantage of these free resources.

Consolidate Your Debt

When you're drowning in debt, there is a solution. Instead of writing a separate check for the minimum amount to all of your creditors, all that unsecured debt (debt that doesn't have a sellable item, like a house or a car, attached to it) can be turned into one payment—usually at a much lower interest rate—that you can more easily manage each month. This is what debt consolidation is all about.

Debt consolidation is not a loan, nor is it a forgiveness of your debts. You pay off all your debts in due time. However, debt consolidation often offers a lower interest rate than you're currently being charged, and if your debts are with collection agencies that expect immediate payment, you may be able to take more time to pay those debts. The best part is that the harassing phone calls and letters will stop immediately.

Usually, you sign an agreement in which you allow your credit counselor to contact your creditors, let your counselor submit a budget on your behalf, agree to make your new payment on time (or have your payments automatically withdrawn from your checking or savings account), and agree not to get into further debt. If your creditors agree (and they usually do), you're usually in a position to be free of these debts in two to five years, provided your budget allows for this. (Your credit counselor will put you on a tight budget until your debt is paid off.)

Use an Accredited Agency

Most, but not all, debt consolidation is performed by credit-counseling agencies. Before you sign on with any agency, check with the National Foundation for Credit Counseling, the Justice Department, and the Better Business Bureau.

Remember that not all credit counselors are the same. Credit card companies have always appreciated credit-counseling services that help people figure out how to pay back their debts, even if it takes them a long time.

This is because when cardholders file for the alternative—bankruptcy—credit card companies often get no payment at all. So, to help these debt-restructuring organizations, credit card companies sometimes donate a percentage of the card balance to the credit-counseling service, often called a "fair share."

Some entrepreneurs, hungry for the fair-share fee, have started businesses as credit counselors. But these companies often push the consumer to pay the credit card companies first—or worse, will work only with debts owed to creditors that pay a fair share—which may not be in your best interest.

Examine the Fee—If Any—for Debt Consolidation

Most organizations charge a nominal fee for debt consolidation: both a setup charge and a monthly fee. Expect this, but the Better Business Bureau (BBB) suggests that you not pay more than $75 for setup and $40 per month. Especially with nonprofit debt consolidation, the money goes to a good cause—paying the agency's considerable expenses to offer low-cost services to their clients—and because of the lower interest rates they'll negotiate on your behalf, you'll still save a bundle of money.

Review the Terms of Your Agreement

Be sure you read the terms of your agreement carefully. You'll usually be expected to make your monthly payment on time—with no exceptions—and you'll also agree not to get into any more debt. This is a bit of tough love because, ultimately, you can't break your cycle of debt if your credit-counseling agency bails you out and then you get right back into debt again. Because they're going to all the trouble of intervening on your behalf, you have to agree to change your lifestyle. It's a tall order, but it's the only way most credit-counseling agencies will work.

Consolidate Your Debts on Your Own

Another way to consolidate your debts is to use one of your credit cards to pay off all your other debts. Many credit cards even provide checks or special forms that help simplify this process, although the fee is usually 3 percent of your balance, which can add up.

Under most circumstances, consolidating this way—on your own and without the guidance and support of a counselor—isn't a good idea. Because you won't have signed an agreement not to rack up any more debt, you may be tempted to use your now-paid-off credit cards to spend more money, making your situation worse.

Also, even if one of your credit cards is offering a low-interest rate to transfer the balances from your other cards to theirs, the rate is usually good only for a limited amount of time (like six months) and may skyrocket after that. A credit counselor can usually arrange for an even lower interest rate for your debts—and it won't expire.

Sell Some Assets

Besides debt consolidation, there is another way to raise money to pay off your debts: Sell some of your assets. If your house, apartment, storage unit, or parent's house is stocked with items belonging to you that you no longer use, and that may have some resale value, consider selling them and using the money to pay down your debts.

Don't confuse pawnshops with tag sales, where you drag out all your stuff and try to make a few bucks. Let's be clear: The people who run pawnshops are nearly always loan sharks, often charging as much as 30 percent annual interest. Steer clear!

Sell Valuable Items

Items that you may be able to sell—and that may be valuable—include furniture, jewelry, fashion items, an automobile or motorcycle, exercise equipment, recreational toys (pool table, bike), paintings, signed books, newer computer equipment, guns, memorabilia (baseball cards, signed sports balls), coin or stamp collections, and outdoor equipment (grill, riding mower).

Whatever items you plan to sell, make sure they're in excellent condition if you expect a high price for them. If they're not nearly new, consider holding a tag sale.

You can sell valuable items in a variety of ways:

- Visit a reputable dealer or consignment shop, specializing in antiques, paintings, guns, jewelry, books, coins, or stamps. If you think your item has some value, see a dealer who resells the type of item you wish to sell or visit a consignment shop specializing in your item.

  Don't visit a pawnshop or any other shady business. Go to the best, highest-class dealer or consignment shop you can find (by searching online and reading reviews) and present your item for sale. If you aren't satisfied with the price, go elsewhere. That particular dealer or shop may simply have too many of what you're trying to sell; another shop may not. (Or you can wait for Antiques Roadshow to visit your city!)

- Auction the item. Your items will have to be fairly valuable to others to warrant a live auction (call a local auction company to arrange an appraisal), but even inexpensive items can be auctioned via online services like eBay (www.ebay.com) or sold on a site specializing in vintage or handmade items like Etsy (www.etsy.com). Visit each site to learn more about their fees, who pays for shipping (usually the buyer, although you'll need to pay for boxing up items), how you can accept payments through PayPal, and to ensure that you've been paid before you ship an item.

- Advertise on Craigslist (www.craigslist.org). Although items on Craigslist tend to fetch a lower price than you'll see in an auction, advertising on Craigslist is free, the buyer will come pick up your item, and your item will likely sell very quickly. Selling your furniture or car on Craigslist can put some quick cash in your pocket, which you can use to pay down your debt.

Hold a Tag Sale

If you own a lot of items, but none is of much value, consider holding a tag sale (also called a yard sale or garage sale). Although your items will sell for much less than you paid for them, you may be able to make hundreds of dollars selling items you consider to be junk. Don't forget, however, that lugging all your items out to the garage or yard, marking them with prices, and being anchored to your sale for a day or two is time-consuming and challenging.

Be sure to mark the price on every single item and include a range of prices, from 25 cents for old kitchen towels to $40 for a dresser that's in good condition. To attract customers, set out an attention-grabber—an item that's highly unusual or brightly colored—near the end of your driveway. And if you don't think you have enough stuff to attract attention, consider combining a sale with neighbors, friends, or family.

Be sure to advertise your sale on your Facebook page, asking friends to share your event to get the word out. You can also advertise on your local paper's website: For a small fee (generally $15–$30, but it could be higher, depending on your location), your sale will be advertised a few days in advance (in the paper and online), and you may even receive some signs to place near your house, at intersections, or on busier streets, showing shoppers how to find you. Your listing should include directions, hours, a list of items, and whether you'll hold your sale in the event of rain.

Expect early birds to arrive from sixty to ninety minutes before your posted time. If you're not ready to open, ignore them and reiterate that you'll be opening at the time listed in the paper. Most of these early shoppers are antique or resale-shop dealers who want the pick of your litter. If you let them in early, regular folks who saw your ad and thought it'd be fun to go to a garage sale may be furious with you.

Get change (a roll of quarters plus small bills) the day before the sale, and during the sale, keep your moneybox in your hands at all times. A common scam is for one person to distract you while another steals your moneybox. Also, if you're not good at addition, keep a calculator nearby.

Cash in Savings Bonds or Stocks

If you own bonds or stocks that aren't earmarked for your (or your child's) education or your retirement and they are valuable, consider cashing them in to pay down your debt. Before deciding, visit your local bank or stockbroker to determine the value of these assets, as well as any penalties and other costs or commissions associated with selling them.

Declare Bankruptcy

Bankruptcy generally isn't a good idea. Although it probably seems much easier than credit counseling, or selling some of your belongings, it can haunt you for a good portion of your life. Think of it this way: Would you ever loan money to a friend who once borrowed from you but never paid it back?

Lenders don't want to do that either, including those that loan money for cars and homes and those that offer unsecured loans like credit cards and store charge cards. You may even have trouble getting the utilities (like electric, gas, and cable) hooked up if you've declared bankruptcy. This means you'll have to prepay these services until you establish a good payment record.

CHAPTER 9

ADD INCOME

If you've reduced your expenses as much as you can and still have trouble finding the money to reach your financial goals, consider temporarily or permanently adding to your income and putting that money toward your debts or into savings.

Recognize What Additional Work Can Mean for You

Extra work can be both a blessing and a curse. Extra income can help you pay off nagging debts that don't seem to budge any other way. Working a second job can also help you build new skills that could lead to a different full-time job or a new business of your own. And nearly anyone can put up with a crazy schedule for a few weeks or even a couple of months, especially if you know exactly when the long hours will end and can count down the days—and add up your extra income.

But managing a heavy workload isn't easy. You have to juggle your responsibilities at home, your relationships with the people who are important to you, and your need for rest and relaxation with your new requirements on the job.

Before trading in your time for money, be sure you can't cut back on your expenses enough to gain the extra money you need. First, try reducing your monthly financial obligations, then consider adding income only as a last resort.

The following sections help you define the pluses and minuses of additional work, and give you some tips for smoothing the rough road ahead.

New Skills That May Lead to Different Work

One approach to choosing your second job is to look for one that builds your skills in a way that will help further your career. Suppose, for example, that you don't have any computer skills. You see an advertisement for a job that requires fifteen hours of work each week at your local library, shelving books.

But you also know that the library's checkout system is computerized, so at your interview, you ask whether you would be able to spend a few hours a week learning the system and, at some point, helping patrons use the system, too. Within just a few months, you may develop enough computer skills to be able to update your resume and apply for a completely different day job—one that requires a basic knowledge of computers—with your current employer or with a new one.

A Foundation for Starting Your Own Company

If you're hoping to go into business for yourself and want extra income to pay off debts before you start the company, or as a cushion against uncertain income, you can start your business on a very part-time basis-perhaps on evenings and weekends—and build both a client base and a reputation before you go into the business full-time.

Suppose, for example, you're thinking of starting a landscaping company. Using the additional evening daylight hours in the summer months, you could begin your landscaping business during evenings and weekends. Let your co-workers, friends, and neighbors know about your new business, and let word spread about your great product or service. Then, as your business picks up, you can begin to cut down your hours at your other job or quit that job altogether.

Besides landscaping, some business ideas that might lend themselves to evenings and weekends include catering, photography, graphic design, website design, furniture refinishing and repair, selling antiques, home remodeling and repair, closet and room organizing, dog training, tutoring, selling cosmetics, and so on.

This is by no means an exhaustive list.

Recently, a baker decided he had developed enough of a clientele during his evenings and weekends to pursue his passion full-time. To get the word out about his service, he submitted his resignation letter, discussing how much he had enjoyed his job and coworkers, on a cake that he had decorated! Of course, that let everyone at work know that he was starting a desserts business, and that meant he grew his clientele before he ever left the job, yet didn't sever any ties with his employer.

Far Less Available Time

The hours you spend working more will have to come from somewhere. Unless you have hours and hours of unfilled free time right now, your additional work is probably going to keep you from spending time with your family, running errands, exercising, futzing with your house or car, visiting friends and extended family, taking a vacation, working on your hobby, reading, playing with your pets, and so on.

This isn't trivial—remember the saying, "All work and no play makes Jack a dull boy"? Working too much can dull your senses, making life seem as though it revolves around work, when, in fact, a healthful life revolves around the people and events that make you happy.

If you're planning to add extra income for a short time—say, until your $6,500 credit card debt is paid off—you can plan ahead with friends and family, agreeing, perhaps, that they'll help you by running some of your errands while you're working to pay off this debt. You may also be able to agree that as soon as the debt is paid off, you'll quit earning the extra income and immediately spend more time with them, maybe even by taking a low-cost, but well-deserved, vacation.

Although the thought of extending your extra income indefinitely may seem like a wise financial choice, keep in mind that life isn't all about work—if you do nothing but work and make money, you'll be likely to either lose the valuable parts of your life or burn out on your existing jobs and begin to dread them.

If you're planning to add extra income for a longer time—perhaps taking on a higher-paying job that requires far more working hours—try to find ways to gain back some of your free time. Move closer to work, hire someone to help with errands and chores, exercise or meet with friends before work or during your lunch hour, listen to audiobooks while you drive, take fun vacations, and so on. Then when you're home, you can be fully at the moment, instead of spending your time at home working, thinking about work, or preparing for the next day of work.

For the short term—for a few weeks or months—most people can survive the stress of working two jobs without damaging their health or relationships. But working long hours for many months or years challenges your emotional and physical health. A second job is a short-term solution, not a long-term one.

Added Stress

Working too much will eventually tax you physically and emotionally, and that can make you fatigued, subject to illness and injury, and irritable, none of which makes you a very good companion, parent, or friend. Also, if your work is highly mental in nature, you may suffer mental stress that can rob you of your ability to converse intelligently and work on detailed hobbies or other projects during your downtime.

Change Jobs

One of the simplest ways to increase your income is to look for a new full-time job. In fact, many job counselors advise their clients to look for new work every few years as a way to boost their income (as well as increase their contacts within the industry). If you receive a 3–5 percent raise every year at your current job, you'll have to work about two to three and a half years before your income goes up by 10 percent. But you may be able to get a 10 percent raise next month by getting a job at another company.

One way to boost your income by staying at your existing job is to change shifts. Often, the third shift (which usually runs from somewhere between 10:00 P.M. and midnight and finishes from 6:00 A.M.–8:00 A.M.) pays much more per hour—even as much as 50 cents or a dollar more.

If you do change jobs, however, be sure the new job—with its higher income—doesn't end up costing you more. It could, if the new job is ten miles farther away, requires expensive clothing that must be dry-cleaned, doesn't offer free parking, and so on. Before accepting a job offer, ask detailed questions about your new responsibilities and the costs that may be involved. If your new job is with your existing company, don't shy away from asking these same questions. Different departments within large corporations often require different dress codes and standard equipment.

Get a Second Job

Getting a second job can help boost your income and can be fun at the same time. To make it as enjoyable as possible, try to find work that suits your personality and interests. If, for example, you have a great love of photography or athletics, consider getting a second job at a photographer's studio or at an athletics store or yoga studio.

If you tend to be outgoing, try to find work that allows you to interact with people. If you're shy, consider working behind the scenes at a company that interests you, instead of having to work with people. By matching your personality and interests to your second job, the extra work may not seem as difficult to endure.

Don't let your employee discount get you further into debt. If you work at a yoga studio and find yourself buying thousands of dollars' worth of comfy pants and shirts that you wouldn't normally have purchased, your second job could be little more than a new way to get into debt.

One of the best times to find a second job in retail is during the holidays. Companies hire seasonal employees from the week of Thanksgiving through the New Year. Once January comes, you're usually out of a second job, but if you've worked out well for the company and express interest in continuing to work for them, you may be called back for the next holiday season and at various times throughout the year.

Work Overtime

Unless you're a salaried employee who is expected to work as many hours as necessary to complete your work, you may have opportunities to work overtime at your current job to earn additional income. Although opportunities for overtime are becoming rare, those companies that do offer it may pay time-and-a-half or double for any hours over forty. That can add up to a lot of additional income in just a short amount of time.

Whatever you do, don't count on overtime income for your everyday expenses! Companies are notorious for eliminating all overtime work whenever the economy contracts a little bit. You may be told that you'll be earning extra income for six months, only to find the work eliminated a month into your stint.

Be aware of the overtime commitments that your company may require. Some companies expect you to commit to working overtime for a set period, even six months or a year before they'll allow you to sign on. And the time required may be open-ended so that you're getting home at 7:30 P.M. one day and 9:00 P.M. the next. Before accepting any opportunity for additional income, be sure you're clear on exactly what's involved.

Freelance for Your Own Company

Although freelancing is similar to working overtime because you're doing work outside of your normal working hours for the company you already work for, it's a little different. In general, freelancing involves taking on a project that no one within the company has the time (or the expertise) to complete. It can involve projects from typing a manuscript or sewing a banner to designing a company brochure or catering a company event. You work on the project in your spare time, usually on your own equipment at home.

Some companies don't allow employees to also work as freelancers for the company. Check with your HR department before accepting any freelance gig from anyone other than your own boss.

Freelancing offers many opportunities:

- Freelancing allows you to use your unique skills and talents to earn extra money.
- Freelancing on a particular project doesn't lock you into working extra hours for an indefinite period.
- Freelancing can improve your reputation with your current employer, especially if you're able to come through on a difficult or time-sensitive project.
- Freelancing can spin off into a full-time gig if you're able to find more clients in addition to your current employer.

Start a Small Business

Every year, over half a million new small businesses launch their products or services. Starting a small business, especially a home-based one, doesn't have to be a full-time investment if you don't want it to be. Instead, if you're trying to find a way to earn extra cash but want some control over how and when you work, starting a small business from your home might be just what you're looking for. The following sections help you answer some important questions about starting a part-time business. WORKSHEET 9-1 can help you determine whether earning extra money by starting a small business is right for you.

WORKSHEET 9-1
BUSINESS EXPENSES

Expense	One-time costs	Monthly costs
	$	$
	$	$
	$	$
	$	$
Total	$	$

Find the Best Small Business for You

The best small business for you is the one that you're enthusiastic and passionate about. This means that your business idea has to mesh with your skills, unique qualities, and personality. If for example, you're thinking about starting a catering business but don't enjoy cooking, you probably won't succeed. If on the other hand, you've always loved cosmetics, and you like dealing with people one-on-one, you might want to try your hand as an Avon, Mary Kay, or Arbonne beauty products consultant.

Matching your work to your personality, qualities, and skills are the topic of hundreds of books. If you're unsure which, a business idea will work best for you, take a trip to your local library or its website and find books that offer self-tests and ideas about home-based businesses.

Determine Whether You're Passionate about Your Business Idea

Finding out whether you're passionate about a business idea is pretty simple—just decide whether you agree or disagree with this statement: Now that I've come up with a potential business, the thought of not pursuing it seems impossible.

If you agree, you're plenty passionate. But if you disagree—that is, if you think your business concept is just okay or seems like too much work—don't bother pursuing it; you won't have the energy required to make it succeed.

Estimate Your Potential Income and Expenses

Estimating your potential income and expenses is always difficult. To keep the number realistic, come up with three scenarios for both income and expenses: best case, average case, and worst case. If, for example, you think you can get three catering jobs per month, use that as your best case, but also figure out how much you'll make with just two catering jobs (average case) or one (worst case).

Do the same with your income. If you're planning to offer graphic-design services from your home and will rely heavily on your Mac, figure in the cost of software updates, attending conferences, and maintaining your own website in your best-case scenario.

Keep in mind that many small-business owners underestimate how much expenses really cost. If you're running a business part-time, you may not need to purchase anything. On the other hand, you may find that you need to set up and maintain a website and social media channels, buy some basic office equipment, invest in business equipment, get inventory for your business, secure a booth at a local tech show, and so on. Whatever equipment will be essential to your business's

success, include it in your worst-case scenario. And then use WORKSHEET 11-2 to estimate your business expenses.

Keep Your Overhead Low

After you think of all the possible equipment you'll need to make your business a success, determine which items would just be nice, which are absolutely necessary, and which you can buy secondhand. Too many first-time business owners spend tens of thousands of dollars outfitting their offices, only to find that those expenses don't increase business traffic one bit!

You can use the basic principles in this book to create a separate budget just for your business. But make sure you include all the "hidden costs"—don't underestimate the cost of hosting your website, buying specialized equipment, and running an office or studio.

Suppose you decide that you don't need a fancy desk for your office—a small wooden one will do just fine. You read the classifieds and look through sale flyers from office-equipment stores and find one that's just $75. That's a few hundred less than a new desk would cost, so it's a good deal, right? Well, no, not if your business doesn't require a desk. If you can do your paperwork at the kitchen table, don't bother buying a desk until you find that you really need one.

Understand Business Taxes

Too many small businesses have folded because their owners failed to estimate their taxes properly. The federal government (and, possibly, your state government, too) requires you to pay approximately one-quarter of the taxes your business will owe for the year's income at four separate times throughout the year: April 15, June 15, September 15, and January 15.

This is known as the "pay as you go" system.

To make these tax payments, you'll need to estimate how much you'll owe in taxes at the end of the year, divide that amount by four, and send a check for that amount by each due date. If you fail to do so, you may have to pay the penalty when you submit your next tax return.

Decide Whether You're Ready

If you check off all of the following questions, starting a small business will probably be right for you:

- You're passionate about your business idea.
- You have the expertise and skills required to do this job well.
- You have a reputation in your community as someone who can be trusted to do a good job.
- You've estimated your expenses and income and feel that the business will bring in the extra income you need.
- Your business idea doesn't require a lot of up-front cash.
- You're willing to spend a lot of time getting your business off the ground.

- You can continue to excel at your full-time job while running your part-time business.
- You don't mind completing a few hours of paperwork once a month or so.
- You're disciplined enough to work during evenings and weekends, even when no one is looking over your shoulder or pressuring you to do it.
- Your family is enthusiastic about your business and wants to help.

CHAPTER 10

STICK TO YOUR BUDGET IN AN EMERGENCY

Too often, a budget gets derailed because of an unexpected expense, especially during the first few months. Ideally, you want to keep money in savings for such emergencies, but in case you haven't had time to build up your cash reserves, here are some ideas for sticking to your budget, even in the worst of times.

If Your Car Breaks Down

Most people on a tight budget have one prayer: "Please don't let anything happen to my car." That's because car repairs can cost hundreds or even thousands of dollars, and you often can't get back and forth to work without a car. So what do you do if your car does break down?

Immediately Find a Way to Get to Work

Whether you have to arrange for a ride from a coworker, ride a bike, take the bus, rent a car, or walk, if you're in an accident or your car isn't running, figure out a way to get to and from work without delay. Too many jobs have been lost because an employee couldn't get to work for three or four days and an employer wasn't very understanding. If you have to miss or be late for even one day of work because of your car, call your supervisor and explain that you have car problems and are trying to find an alternate way to work right away.

Consider alternate ways to get to and from work before your car breaks down. Even if you never have a bit of trouble with your car, you'll have the peace of mind that comes from knowing how you'd handle a car crisis if you had one.

Research Your Warranty and Insurance Coverage

If you recently bought a new car and your troubles aren't due to an accident, your car is probably under warranty and will be repaired for free. Even if you bought the car used, you may have a short-term warranty that covers the repairs you need.

If, on the other hand, your car isn't running because of an accident, call your insurance company to determine how much of the repairs your policy will pay for.

Get a Free Repair Estimate

If you can get your car to a repair shop, take it there and ask for a free, no-commitment estimate. Make sure you emphasize the "free" and "no-commitment" parts of the estimate. Many repair shops don't charge for estimates as long as you end up repairing your car there. If you decide not to repair it, or if you go somewhere else for the repair, they'll bill you $50 or $100 for the estimate! Be sure to let the repair shop know that you're on a very tight budget and need to know the least expensive way to get your car running again.

If you can't get your car to a garage or repair shop without towing it (which can be very expensive), call a few garages and describe the problems you're having. Tell them about your tight budget and ask for a ballpark estimate for the problems you're describing.

Call Around to Compare Your Price

After you know what the problem is, call several garages in your area (or go online) to find out what they will charge for the same repair. Emphasize that you need to know the total amount and can't afford any surprises. If they won't give you a price, call somewhere else.

If you're going to have it repaired and can't drive it, also call several towing companies to find out how much they'll charge to tow your car to the shop. Keep in mind that your insurance company, travel club, or cell phone provider may also offer free towing in a limited area. Find this out before you call a tow truck.

Some car repairs are simple enough to do yourself. If you or a friend or family member knows anything about cars, consider buying the parts and fixing the problem yourself. As long as you have an alternative way to work every day, you can spend a few hours each evening working on your car until it's repaired.

Will the Shop Let You Pay over Time?

When you find the repair shop that has the best prices and can get the job done quickly, find out whether it'll let you pay over time, say, in three or four payments, without charging interest. The shop may say no, but it's worth asking.

Develop a New Budget

Using the repair estimates, develop a new budget. Do you have money in savings that you can use? Can you pay the shop a little each month? Can you make the repairs yourself? Can you live without a car and walk, bike, or carpool to work? Can you buy a new-to-you car and still stick with your budget?

Investigate every possible option, but be realistic in your numbers. Whatever route you decide to take—whether that's to make the repair, get another car, or find a way to do without—use your revised budget to begin working toward your financial goals again.

If You Incur Extensive Household Expenses

Although you can put off some household repairs, others are critical. If the roof leaks, the sewer drain is clogged, the water isn't running, or you've lost electric power to some of your rooms, you need to get them repaired or replaced. These repairs, however, can be expensive!

"1100

MAY 9th
GOALS

50,000 Net egg
over. 16 years.

3 monts of Bills
10,000

Teeth.   2 YeAr
          PlAn.
30,000

House   5 Year
          PlAn
300.000
New CAR.   8 Year
           PlAn
           8 Years
F   COSt   10,00

$400 mon.

$8,000 4 years

2 G

10,000

30,000   10

10

11 7

10

7

The first thing you want to do is try to fix the problem temporarily so that the repair doesn't blossom into something bigger. Can you, for example, stop a leak by going up into the attic and putting plastic under some of the deckings to stop water from coming in? Can you clean out the sewer line with a snake (available from any hardware store)? Have you called the water company to see whether the problem is on its side (that is, in the lines leading up to your water meter)?

Ultimately, however, you're going to have to make one of two choices: sell the house with the problem or fix the problem. The next two sections discuss these two options.

Sell the House

One way to get out from under large, expensive repairs is to sell your house and move to a smaller one. The problem, of course, is that either you'll have trouble selling the house to any buyer or you'll have trouble selling it for very much money. One way to avoid losing too much money is to price the house as though the repair did not have to be made (as if the roof were in great condition, for example), and advertise up-front that you'll give back half (or two-thirds, or all) of the amount necessary to make the repair at closing. You won't actually have to come up with that cash out of your savings or another account.

Instead, that amount will be subtracted from your equity (the amount of your house that you have paid off) and given to the buyer as a lump sum. You'll get that much less money from selling your house, but you're likely to get more buyers than if you simply price the house lower in the first place. Why? Because many buyers can't afford to make large repairs—they're using all of their cash reserves for the down payment. But if you give cash back at closing, your buyer will have the cash to make the repair.

If you're thinking of selling your house, keep in mind that not every house sale requires the use of a real-estate agent. Because agents get 6–7 percent of the selling price of the house, if you don't hire one, you can afford to do a lot of advertising and pay for an attorney or Realtor to draw up the paperwork (which usually costs $500–$1,500) and still come out ahead. Many people use real-estate agents because they believe they'll get a higher price for their homes—after all, Realtors get a higher commission if the house sells for more money. But even this may not be true.

Some Realtors would rather sell a house cheaply and quickly than price it high and wait for it to sell. If they have to wait an extra three months—and do quite a bit more work showing and advertising the house—to sell it at a higher price, they could actually lose money; they'd rather sell it three months earlier for less money and put cash in your hand.

Keep in mind, however, that if you act as your own agent, you'll have to put up a sign, take out online ads, and show the house yourself, and you won't have a Realtor to turn to for advice along the way. Use your best judgment. If you take some time to read up on how to sell your own house and think you're up to the task, go for it. If you don't think you'll be successful at selling your own home, shop around for a good Realtor.

Pay for the Repair (but How?)

If you have money in your savings account, even if it was earmarked for something else, you probably want to use it to pay for your home repairs. Short of that, the most logical way to pay for overwhelming household repairs is to refinance your home and cash out some of the equity to pay for the repair.

Even if you don't have much equity in your house (to find your equity, subtract the amount owing on your mortgage from the amount your house is worth), you may have enough to help with the repairs. But be aware of how doing so can hurt you:

- Your monthly payments may soar. (On the other hand, if interest rates are lower than when you bought your house, your monthly payments may stay the same.)
- You may not have any equity in your house if you plan to sell it in a few years.

You never want to finance your home for more than you can sell it for. If your income changes, you might be trapped in your home, unable to sell it and unable to afford the payments.

If Family Medical Bills Overwhelm You

Even if you carry medical insurance, unexpected medical bills can pile up. Here's why. Suppose your insurance carries a $250 deductible and then pays 80 percent of your medical expenses (your 20 percent is called your copayment). You are in a car accident that doesn't do any permanent damage to your body, but it does result in $15,000 in hospital bills. Of that $15,000, you'll owe $250 for your deductible and $2,950 for your copayment, for a total of $3,200! Where in the world are you going to come up with that?

You have only one option: Work out a payment plan with the hospital. (A second option is to pay the bill with your credit card and pay it off aggressively each month, but often the interest rate on credit cards is sky-high.) Some hospitals offer interest-free payments if you pay within three to six months; others charge interest (but usually less than credit card companies charge) no matter how soon you pay.

Never ignore payment notices from a hospital or doctor's office. So many people do this that medical providers are quick to turn to collection agencies and send negative reports to credit-reporting agencies. You may damage your credit rating for years to come.

Most medical providers are willing to work with you to pay off a large balance. They need to know immediately, however, that you'll have trouble paying the balance and want to set up a payment plan.

If you're not sure how much you can pay, revisit your budget. Eliminate any expenses that aren't required, and see how much you may be able to eke out each month. If this isn't enough, try larger-scale ways to cut your expenses.

When you've determined how much you can afford to pay each month, approach the medical provider with this amount to see whether it's acceptable. You may have to sign an agreement saying that you'll pay this amount each month—be sure you can pay it before you sign. Remember: Check your budget first. If the medical provider gives you a monthly amount, don't agree until you've run the numbers on your budget.

If You Become Sick or Disabled—Even Temporarily

If you're in an accident or develop an illness that leaves you disabled even for a short period, call your employer immediately. Most employers carry disability insurance on their employees that ranges from 40 to 80 percent of your income, and most can offer you some pay for sick time until that insurance kicks in.

Send your human resources (HR) representative every bit of information he or she needs to process your claim, including a letter from your physician that outlines your inability to work.

Whatever you do, don't react to the stress of the situation by getting defensive with your employer. Your HR rep should feel as though you're as horrified at your absence as the company is and that you can't wait to get back to work. Keep in mind that a small number of employees fake illness and injury to collect disability pay without working, and you don't want to be labeled as someone who is trying this scam. If the company doesn't believe that you're disabled, you could lose more than a few weeks' pay—you could lose your job. You might be able to fight it in court, but that takes money, too. Instead, contact your employer immediately and work to resolve your problem.

Even if your company carries disability insurance, however, it may not kick in for some time, and when it does, it won't give you 100 percent of your pay. In this case—or if your company does not carry disability insurance—take the same actions that you would if you lost your job.

If You Lose Your Job

If you're laid off from your job, you'll probably feel angry, overwhelmed, and out of control, but this is an important time to stay calm. Not only will you need to keep your wits about you to make the best possible financial decisions, but you'll also want to watch what you say to coworkers, supervisors, and company representatives.

You never know when someone you work with now will land at a company you apply to later; you'll want to keep your reputation intact so that you have as many future networking opportunities as possible.

If a Friend or Family Member Needs Assistance

Many people are in financial trouble because they've given a friend or family member financial assistance that they clearly cannot afford: making a loan that isn't paid back, offering free room and board, buying a car for someone. Don't let this happen to you.

If a friend or family member is in need, you absolutely must help. But, if possible, avoid helping financially unless you can afford to lose that money completely.

Always assume that loans won't be paid back or will be defaulted on, expenses associated with free room and board will be completely on your shoulders, and so on. If you can't afford to lose the amount of money that helping your friend will cost, don't help financially. Offer prayers, free babysitting (for a limited period), a ride to work until a car is repaired, free tutoring on your area of expertise, and so on.

Also consider taking your friend to a credit-counseling agency, or to a lender, to see about getting financial assistance. Don't, however, cosign any loan that you cannot afford to pay off yourself.

If a Natural Disaster Strikes

What happens when a hurricane, tornado, earthquake, fire, or flood displaces you from your home, closes down your place of employment, or submerges your car underwater? The question can be answered in two ways: what you do before disaster strikes, and what you do after.

Preparing for a Disaster

The best way to prepare for a disaster is to assume it will happen to you someday and make plans accordingly. Here are a few tips:

- Review your insurance coverage and videotape your belongings. Natural disasters are no longer outliers; they can and do happen with increasing frequency, so make sure your homeowner's, renter's, and/or auto insurance will cover both the damage from such disasters and allow for temporary housing or a vehicle if you need them. Also, make a digital video of the contents of your entire home, and keep one copy on your phone or computer and another in the cloud—or make a DVD and store it in a safe-deposit box. I have two friends who lost all their possessions from Hurricane Sandy and didn't have insurance to cover their losses or videos of their belongings. Both have struggled to get any help from the Federal Emergency Management Agency (FEMA) or local agencies and have had to start over.

- Strive to save six months of income for emergencies. Although you'll find this advice throughout this book, it bears repeating here: Start saving now, even if it's just $5 per week. Your goal is to have six months of living expenses in the bank to use if you lose your job, become disabled, or are displaced in a disaster.

- Keep a backup of all your files in the cloud and on a backup hard drive. Losing your computer is generally less of a blow than losing your files, so keep a backup of financial documents, tax returns, favorite photos, journals, and creative work. Keep a physical backup as well as cloud storage so that, if the servers go down for your cloud files, you still have access to your files on your hard drive, and if your hard drive doesn't make it out with you, you still have access to your cloud files.

- Purchase a waterproof, fireproof box ($35–$50) or sign up for a safe-deposit box at your bank ($25–$50 per year). Either option allows you to keep important documents safe during a flood or fire. You can also scan documents and keep them in digital form, but some documents, like a marriage license or the title to your car, need to be kept in hardcopy.

- Trust weather reports and evacuation notices. Living through Hurricane Sandy reinforced for me that over preparation is better than under preparation.
- Keep a go-bag ready. Here's what you do. Go to a resale shop, purchase a sturdy backpack, and fill it with the following: flashlight and extra batteries; nonperishable food items like nuts, crackers, granola bars, and jerky; a few bottles of water; phone charger(s); copies of insurance policies; a list of bank and credit-card account numbers and each bank's contact information; $100–$200 in cash; toothbrushes and toothpaste; sunscreen; gloves and hats. Also, consider adding other items that make sense for your situation and geographic location.

Keep your go-bag in a closet near your front door. In the event of a disaster, have a plan for quickly scooping up other items that you'll add to your bag: your phone, backup hard drive, small electronics like a laptop or tablet, favorite toys for your kids, prescription drugs, rain gear, car keys, and wallets. Once or twice a year, practice how quickly you can get these items into your go-bag and get everyone, including pets, out the door. You might also want to keep some basic camping equipment, blankets, a few gallons of bottled water, and additional nonperishable food in the trunk of your car.

Cleaning Up After a Disaster

If you've had the chance to prepare for a disaster, your cleanup will go much more smoothly than if you're unprepared and don't have copies of your insurance policies, a list of creditors' phone numbers, a go-bag, phone chargers, and cash on hand. But even the best preparation won't get you back into your home if it has been damaged or destroyed by a natural disaster.

Fortunately, communities and the Red Cross tend to respond to disasters quickly and efficiently, setting up temporary shelters, charging stations, FEMA paperwork and interview areas, and other assistance ranging from clothing to meals. Take advantage of everything that's offered, even if it means standing in long lines or filling out complicated paperwork. Your goal will be to get back on sure financial footing as quickly as possible and not let this unfortunate situation force you to start over.

CHAPTER 11

SAVE FOR RETIREMENT

The information here will get you thinking about saving for retirement, but it only scratches the surface. Dig deeper by reading online sites that are devoted to the topic of retirement planning, taking seminars on the subject, and/or meeting with a financial planner.

Figure Out How Much You'll Need

This is the million-dollar question: How much money will you need in retirement? Unfortunately, there is no set answer. How much you'll need depends on your expenses during your retirement years. If, for example, you will no longer have a house payment or rent in retirement, you may be able to live on a lot less than if you must continue to make those payments. On the other hand, if you live in an older house in retirement, you may also encounter more repairs than someone in a new condo.

No one has the ability to look into a crystal ball and know exactly what your expenses will be. The best you can do is an estimate, make adjustments, estimate a little more closely, make more adjustments, and on and on!

The main reason people put off saving for retirement is that they think they have plenty of time to do that later. The second most common reason for putting it off is that most people don't know how to come up with money to put into savings. If you've read the first part of this book, though, you can probably come up with a variety of ways to find $50, $100, or $200 a month for retirement savings.

Ideas for reducing your current expenses

Stop Eating Out

If you eat take-out twice a week, and you pay $14 for a meal that you could make for $4 at home, you could put about $80 a month into your retirement savings. Over twenty years at 2 percent, that's $23,623. As interest rates rise, you'll save even more.

Cut Your Clothing and Shoe Budget in Half

If you spend $1,000 per year on clothing and shoes, can you cut that amount in half and put $500 a year ($42 per month) into a retirement account? Thirty years of that at 3 percent, and you'll have $24,536 to add to your retirement account.

Move to a Smaller House

If you're currently living with two other people in 2,400 square feet, could you move to a house with 1,800 square feet and still be comfortable? What about 1,200 square feet? If so, your mortgage payment might go down from $1,500 to $500 per month. You could put that money into a retirement fund. In just fifteen years at 3 percent, an $800-per-month savings will equal a whopping $182,032.

Another way to get more money for retirement is to refinance your mortgage when interest rates decline. For the cost of closing the loan, you might be able to find an extra $75–$200 per month for your retirement savings. Just don't increase the length of the loan, though, or you'll sacrifice your long-term financial health.

Drive Your Car Twice as Long

If you currently get a new car every three years, pay it off, and buy another new one, try something different: Pay off your car in three years but drive it for six. Put the amount of your car payment into a retirement account for the second three years. You'll only contribute to your retirement account three years out of every six, but you'll have found a creative way to save.

Start a Part-Time Business

Instead of looking only at potential expenses to cut, consider working a few extra hours per week, perhaps at your own business, and putting that income toward your retirement savings. There are ways to earn a bit more money than you're making now.

Look at Tax-Deferred Ways to Save

When most people think of retirement and the government at the same time, they think of Social Security, the government program that collects money from you throughout your working life and gives it back to you, one month at a time, during your retirement years.

If you're nearing retirement, you can probably count on quite a bit of Social Security income for your retirement. If you haven't already, you will soon receive a statement that explains how much you'll receive each month, based on exactly what age you retire.

If you're, say, forty or younger, however, there isn't much chance that Social Security will fully fund your retirement. That's because instead of taking income from you, investing that income, charging a small administrative fee, and then paying you benefits from the investment, the system actually works quite differently.

The money you paid in isn't there anymore: What you paid in ten years ago was used to pay benefits to other people ten years ago; what you paid in last week was used to pay benefits to other people last week. That worked pretty well when the largest generation in American history (baby boomers) was working. But as they enter retirement, the government will probably not be able to collect enough in Social Security income to offset the benefits being paid to boomers.

If you're forty or younger, don't count on Social Security to be a part of your retirement package. The money may not be available when it's time for you to draw out the earnings you put in. If it is, that'll be a bonus!

As a result, the government has taken two steps: increasing the age at which you can begin to draw Social Security benefits, and encouraging you to invest more money in your own retirement accounts to use when you retire. The following sections give you some examples of how they hope to encourage you to do that.

Traditional IRA

An individual retirement account (IRA) is a voluntary retirement savings plan. Up to certain limits, you can contribute to an IRA every year and deduct the amount of your contribution from your federal income taxes. Starting at age fifty-nine and a half, you can withdraw funds from your IRA each month. At that time, the money you withdraw is taxed, but because you'll probably be at a lower tax level, you'll still save tax dollars. Withdrawing the money before age fifty-nine and a half results in substantial penalties. Also, you must begin receiving disbursements from your traditional IRA at age seventy and a half.

You can make an IRA contribution as late as the day your taxes are due (usually April 15) and still credit your IRA contribution to the previous year's taxes. As long as you're making money doing something, in 2013 you can deposit $5,500 into a traditional IRA (as long as you make at least that amount in income), and that number will likely go up, as it has (gradually) for the last decade.

You may also be limited in traditional IRA contributions if your company sponsors a retirement plan for you, even if you don't participate, or if your spouse is covered by a retirement plan at work. Consult IRS documents at www.irs.gov to determine those contribution limitations.

Roth IRA

A Roth IRA is a variation of a traditional IRA, but the tax benefits of the plans are in total opposition. With a Roth IRA, instead of getting a tax deduction for your contribution now and paying tax on the amount distributed to you in retirement, you get no tax deduction now, but you pay no tax on the money distributed to you later. Like a traditional IRA, you can contribute $5,500 per year in 2013.

Also like a traditional IRA, however, you can't contribute if you earn too much money ($127,000 for single incomes; $188,000 for joint incomes in 2013), and if you earn $112,000–$127,000 for singles ($178,000 and $188,000 for joint filers), the amount you can contribute is less than the full allowable amount.

A Roth IRA does have a couple of benefits over traditional IRAs, though. One is that you can continue to contribute as long as you'd like and do not have to begin taking distributions at age seventy and a half. The other is that you can contribute to a Roth IRA even if your company sponsors a retirement plan.

SEP-IRA

A Simplified Employee Pension (SEP) IRA works like a traditional IRA, but it's set up by an employer for its employees . . . and that means you, if you're self-employed, even if you don't have any employees. Really, if you're self-employed, a SEP-IRA is a fantastic way to save quickly for retirement. As long as the employer (you) does not offer another retirement plan, the employer (you) can contribute up to 25 percent of an employee's (your) income into the SEP-IRA every year.

You can take the account with you when leaving the company (that is, your company) to take another job. All of the money contributed comes from the employee's (your) income, but it's not taxed until you receive it during your retirement years, as long as you're over fifty-nine and a half.

Let Your Employer Help You

For most of the twentieth century, companies paid the retirement incomes of their long-term employees, so the employees didn't have to worry about saving for their retirement years. My, how times have changed in the twenty-first century! Most employees do not stay with companies long enough to be considered long term, and most companies do not provide any of their own money to fund retirement accounts. There are a few exceptions, however, discussed in the following sections.

Pension Plan

Your company places money into a retirement account (the

amount contributed on your behalf depends on your income, age, and years of service), manages that account, and pays benefits to you from that account when you retire. When you receive distributions from a pension plan (either monthly, annually, or in a lump-sum payment), you're taxed on the income.

Profit Sharing/401(k)/403(b)/457

In this type of plan, your company contributes money, tax-free, into an individual account on your behalf based on how much you ask to have contributed from your salary (the IRS set a limit of $17,500 in 2013, as long as you made at least that much in income). Some companies match all or part of these contributions, making your potential annual contribution quite high.

Distributions at retirement are taxed.

401(k) plans are used at for-profit companies; 403(b) plans are used at religious, educational, and charitable organizations; 457 plans are used for employees of state and local governments.

SIMPLE IRA

A Savings Incentive Match Plan for Employees (SIMPLE) IRA is similar to a traditional IRA and a SEP-IRA. A SIMPLE IRA is set up by a business with fewer than 100 employees (including yours, if you own a small business). Contribution limits to a SIMPLE IRA are currently $12,000 and increase each year.

The employer then matches a portion of your contribution—usually, a dollar-for-dollar match—for up to 3 percent of your income, or the employer makes a non-matching contribution of 2 percent of your income.

Employee Stock Ownership Plan

An employee stock ownership plan (ESOP) is a retirement account made up mostly of company stock paid for by your employer and, potentially, added to with purchases of company stock that you make. ESOPs can be difficult to take with you if you leave the company, but they can often be transferred into company stock or cash.

To find out what your company has to offer, visit the human resources department and ask questions about what's available. You won't have to commit to a plan at that point, but you can use the information to see how much you can save for your retirement with a contribution that's automatically withdrawn from your paycheck.

Keep in mind that your ESOP is worth only what your company's stock is worth. If you have any doubts about whether your company will still be in business when you retire, don't count on the money from your ESOP as retirement income.

Invest on Your Own

In addition to putting away retirement savings in tax-deferred or company-sponsored plans, you can always save and invest on your own. Remember, however, that you should first take advantage of any free money your employer might be offering in retirement-matching plans, then take advantage of tax-deferred retirement plans, and only as a third choice begin a simple savings account or a more complex investment portfolio for your retirement income.

Saving money in a savings account is quite simple and doesn't require any particular knowledge or skill. You may want to periodically shift your savings to a high-yield savings account, long-term CD, or a savings bond to earn a higher interest rate.

Investing, which is significantly more complicated than stashing your money in a savings account, requires some knowledge of the markets, company documents, and trading rules. If you're interested in learning more about investing, do it. If you're conservative in your investments and take time to read all the available financial documents on companies in which you're investing, the risk is far smaller than most people believe. If you have no interest in doing this, hire a stockbroker or financial consultant to invest for you.

Start Young

The absolute best way to save for retirement is to start young. If you start saving $100 per month when you're twenty-five, and you invest that in a mutual fund or other stock-related fund that sometimes earns 18-percent interest and sometimes loses money, averaging 8 percent over the next forty years, you'll have $351,428.13 for retirement. To get the same amount of retirement savings if you start at age forty, you'll have to put away about $367 per month. Use the cool calculators at Motley Fool to see how much you'll put away for retirement, just by starting young.

Make Up for Lost Time

Regardless of how old you are, you can still save some money for your retirement thanks to the government's catch-up provision, which allows you to save more money in a retirement account when you're over fifty than when you were younger.

You may also be able to use the equity you've built up in your house to fund part of your retirement. The following two sections share some details about each option.

Use the Catch-Up Provision

If you're over fifty, you're allowed to put away more tax-free income per year than your younger counterparts. For example, while the standard contribution to both traditional and Roth IRAs is $5,500 per year, anyone over fifty can contribute $1,000 more than that. Your company's 401(k) plan has similar provisions, allowing you to contribute more than younger workers. This is called a catch-up provision, and it's meant specifically for people who started saving for retirement later in life.

Use Your House to Help You Retire

If you haven't made many provisions for your retirement and can't seem to find the money to do so, you may be able to tap the value of your house for your retirement. Suppose you're forty-five years old and have fifteen years left to pay on your house. You bought the house fifteen years ago, and home prices have risen significantly, even with the setback during the late 2000s. Your house is worth $240,000 now and will likely be worth over $400,000 when you turn sixty and the house is paid off.

Rather than staying in the house after you retire, you can sell it then and move to a smaller house or condominium that costs far less. If you can sell your house for $400,000 and buy a condo at that time for $250,000 or $300,000, you'll have $100,000 to $150,000 to add to your retirement account.

On the other hand, you can stay in the house and get a reverse mortgage on it as soon as you begin needing income (say, when you turn sixty-five or seventy). With a reverse mortgage, a bank buys the house back from you, except that you continue to own it and live in it. You must be at least sixty-two and own your house free and clear. The bank then either sends you monthly payments or gives you a lump sum.

You'll pay a fee for this service because if you live longer than the bank thinks you're going to live, it may actually lose money on the deal. Still, many lenders offer this option.

CHAPTER 12

STAY MOTIVATED

When your long-term financial goals lead you to cut your expenses to the bone and, potentially, work a second job, you may have trouble staying motivated. Here is some encouragement and inspiration for those tough times.

Stick with Your Budget Through Thick and Thin

The best way to stay motivated when you're weary from saving every spare dime is to have already decided from the get-go that you're going to stick to your budget, no matter what. This discipline—deciding that, no matter who tries to influence you, you're going to reach your financial goals, and not let anything or anyone get you off track—will help keep you strong when temptations arise.

When you're establishing financial goals, avoid words or phrases like "try," "would like to," or "might." Instead, state your goals as strongly as you can: "I will pay off my credit card debt by September of next year," instead of "I'll try to pay off my credit cards" or "I'd like to pay off my credit cards." The primary difference is the attitude you take your ability to control your finances.

Unfortunately, discipline isn't easy, and if you don't make a full commitment to your budget when you establish it, you may find yourself opting for small pleasures now that get you further into debt, put you back in debt after you've gotten out, or simply delay reaching your financial goals for that many more months or years.

Consider deciding now, right this very minute, that you're going to stick to your budget, no matter what.

Make Motivational Signs

To stay motivated to stick to your budget, make inspirational signs for yourself and put them in places around your home where you're likely to see them, and in your wallet. Here are some examples:

- I'm going back to school next year.
- I will retire at age fifty-five.
- I am buying a house next spring.
- I will be out of debt by the last day of June.
- I'm buying my granddaughter a bike for her birthday.

Your signs can say anything you want, as long as they're meaningful to you and address your most important financial goals. Place large ones on your refrigerator and on your bedroom nightstand; tape smaller ones to your coffeemaker and bathroom mirror. Place one in your wallet, wrapped around your credit card, debit card, or cash. Put one on your computer or smartphone. Put one in your car.

Having too many of these signs won't motivate you—they'll just make you laugh! If you find yourself needing signs everywhere to keep you motivated, try making a sign that says, "I will stop making these signs!" That should be fun for a few days.

If You Blow Your Budget—Get Back on Track

Suppose you get off track. You get so tired of austerity that you put your credit card back in your wallet, drive to your local shopping mall, and under the guise of "it's on sale," buy a few hundred dollars' worth of clothes or electronic equipment.

You don't have any way to pay for these purchases, except by taking money out of savings, or worse, by paying your credit card company until the debt is paid off. If this happens, stay calm. Nobody's perfect, and after you've come this far on your financial journey, this small setback won't kill you. You can, however, take some steps toward minimizing the effects of your shopping spree:

1. Don't remove tags or open boxes from any purchases for one week.
2. One week after you buy any item, see how you feel about returning it for a refund.
3. If a refund isn't possible, either because the store won't accept returned merchandise or because you ripped the tags off the minute you got home, see whether a friend or relative wants to buy the item from you at full price.

4. If you're sure, you no longer want the items you purchased but can't return them (as is the case if you bought them from a resale or consignment shop), consider placing the new items on eBay. Brand-new items will fetch a better price than even gently used items up for auction. Be sure, however, to set your initial bid high enough to recoup most of your costs.

5. If a refund or sale isn't possible or if you really want to keep the items, revisit your budget to see how you can pay for them.

Is there a law that makes stores accept returns?

Unfortunately, no. Every business is allowed to set its own return policies, but if a store doesn't accept returns or gives only a store credit, it must tell you this on the receipt, in person, or on visible signs.

You may find that, in order to pay for your splurge, you have to cut back your expenses even further than before or get a part-time job to pay off the debt. If that's the case, do it. Whatever you do, don't go back into debt because of one small slip-up.

Find Sneaky Ways to Spend Money

Finding ways to spend money on yourself now and then is critical to your continuing ability to save and spend wisely. The problem is that treating yourself is usually expensive and can blow your budget. This section gives you some ideas on how you can celebrate your budgeted life in easy and inexpensive ways.

Make a List of Free Activities

Sit down and make a list of free activities that you enjoy. These activities might include watching a certain program on TV, visiting a nearby park, playing in the backyard with your dog, sitting on your porch reading a library book, attending a free concert, taking a bath, and so on.

With this list in hand, treat yourself to one of these activities every time you meet a financial milestone, even if it's just writing out a check to your credit card company for more than the minimum amount due. Because you'll look forward to these free activities, you'll also be motivated to stick to even the most tiresome budget.

Give Yourself Six Dollars to Splurge

Giving yourself such a small amount of money to splurge when you meet your financial goals may not seem very motivating, but you might be amazed at what you can do with $6. You can see a matinee movie, eat lunch at a fast-food restaurant, rent a movie through Redbox and buy two candy bars, purchase a new pair of socks, buy a paperback book, or get a new coffee or tea mug. The point isn't what you do as much as that you do it. With your $6 in hand, you can focus on spending it on the perfect thing for you. And that will tide you over until the next time you can splurge with $6 again.

If your budget allows for a smaller or larger amount than $6 as periodic splurging money, make a list of what you can get with $1 or $10. You can be just as creative with any amount of money.

Reinvigorate Something You Already Own

When you're bogged down with paying off your debts and feel like you need to have something new in your life, consider sprucing up something you already own and giving it to yourself—even wrapping it up as a present! One simple way to do this is to go through your closet and find an article of clothing that you like but haven't worn in a while. Giving it to yourself again will help it seem like a fresh purchase. If it makes your wardrobe seem newer and fresher, you may feel as though you've been treated to something new.

Pretend to Spend

E-commerce sites bemoan "abandoned cart" syndrome: people who shop online and put items into their cart but then never buy. But you can use this same concept to satisfy some of your urge to spend. With your credit and debit cards put away, imagine that you won the lottery and start considering what you would buy—and put those items into online carts or on a list on a notepad.

What would you buy? A new car? A new wardrobe? Electronics? A boat? A house? Whatever it would be, decide exactly what you would buy—but then don't buy it. Just let it sit in your online cart or on your list. Soon, the urge to shop will pass, and you'll be out of the woods.

Warning: If you're not very disciplined, don't try this activity. It might be really fun deciding what to buy, looking at cars, and filling out order forms, but under no circumstances can you actually purchase these items! If you think you might be tempted, choose another idea.

Imagine Yourself Reaching Your Goals

One sure way to motivate yourself is to find a `comfortable spot to sit, and then imagine yourself reaching your financial goals. Visualize yourself sitting in your new house, watching your child's college graduation, being treated to a retirement party at whatever age you decide on, and so on. Do this every time your strict budget gets you down.

Build a Support Network

To stay disciplined and motivated to meet your financial goals, enlist the help of one or two close friends. Begin by summarizing your current financial situation and goals (don't be too specific, just give the highlights), and then ask your friend whether you can call him or her for support from time to time. Just be sure that this is a friend who will help you stick to the plan, not one who will tempt you to abandon your budget and get further away from your financial goals. Choose someone whose spending and saving habits you admire.

Whether by birth, death, or a parent or other family member coming to live with you, changes in your family's size will result in changes in your expenses, and these changes mean that you need a new budget.

A budget tells you how your income and expenses will affect your financial picture, and a new family member may have a significant impact on your ability to meet your financial goals. On the other hand, when your youngest leaves the house, you may find that you have significantly more money to spend or save. Revisiting your budget can help you see where to put this newfound money.

Whenever You Receive an Inheritance or Other Windfall

Your first reaction at receiving any lump sum of money may be to spend, spend, and spend. All that pent-up consumerism may be tempted to run wild with this influx of cash.

Suppose one of your financial goals is to save enough for a 20 percent down payment on a house, and that's going to cost you about $40,000. For the last year, you've been sticking to your budget and have over $6,000 saved.

Now you receive $30,000 from a rich uncle who recently passed away. You think of getting new golf clubs or new furniture, right? Not so fast! Revisit that budget, and you'll find that if you put your inheritance into savings, you're now just $4,000 away from buying that new house. And at the rate you've been saving, you can save that in eight months.

If you use your windfall wisely, you could reach some of your financial goals years, maybe even decades, sooner. But if you spend the money impetuously, you may regret it for years or decades.

Before You Start a Business

Before jumping into any business—whether a small home-based business, a franchise or a partnership with a plush office—run the numbers for your budget. Businesses need time before they become profitable, and only by revisiting your budget can you plan for the lean months.

Whenever Your Goals Shift

Don't be surprised if your goals change as time goes on. One great example of this is how meaningless retirement savings seem to a person in his or her twenties. Even some forty-year-olds are still too far from retirement to care! But the fact is, as your friends and coworkers begin to retire, saving for your own retirement will likely become your number-one financial goal, and you'll attack it with a vengeance.

Your other goals may change, too. Some, like paying off credit cards or buying a house, will disappear because you've reached them. Others, like retiring at age forty or buying a beach house, may simply disappear because you can't cut your expenses or raise your income enough to ever meet those goals. Still others, like paying 100 percent of your kids' college costs, may be replaced with more practical goals, like paying 50 or 75 percent of those costs.

CONCLUSION

Your goals may begin to shift because of the reality that a budget brings to your financial life. If that's the case, accept that certain goals simply aren't possible, and move forward with the ones that are. But other goals may change for other reasons, and you'll need to pull out your budget to see how these new goals can fit into your financial plan. Perhaps, for example, you had originally thought you would retire at age fifty but now have a new goal: to retire from your current job at age fifty and start a new business that you'll work at a part-time until you turn sixty-five. That new goal will have its own expenses and timelines that need to be incorporated into a new budget.

Made in the USA
Coppell, TX
08 April 2021